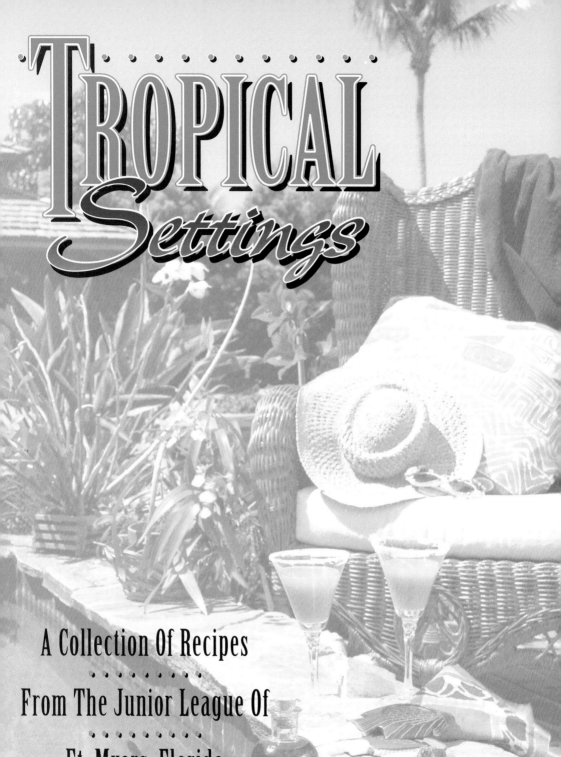

TROPICAL Settings

A Collection Of Recipes

From The Junior League Of

Ft. Myers, Florida

Published by The Junior League of Ft. Myers, Inc.

Edited, Designed and Manufactured by
Favorite Recipes® Press
P.O. Box 305142
Nashville, Tennessee 37230
1-800-358-0560

First Printing: 1995 20,000 copies

Library of Congress Catalog Number 95-61430
ISBN: 0-9613314-1-0

This cookbook is a collection of our favorite recipes, which are not
necessarily original recipes.

Proceeds from the sale of this book will benefit the community
projects of the Junior League of Ft. Myers, Inc.

Additional copies of *Tropical Settings* may be obtained by using the
order form on page 255 or by writing:
The Junior League of Ft. Myers, Inc.
Cookbook Sales
P.O. Box 07341
Ft. Myers, Florida 33919

Cookbook Development Committee

Jody Hart Chairman 1991–1993

Kim Bauman Chairman 1993–1995

Ann Arnall

Wendy Beville

Alexandra Bremner

Annette Capel

Julia Clark

Patricia Clark

Jeana Crevasse

Kathy Eskin

Jan Fryzel

Phyllis Holley

Margot Kenzie

Kim Kuhn

Maggie Lewis

Rebecca McAlpine

Gretchen Nelson

Janet Newman

Bunny Nocera

Donna Pankow

Ann Randolph

Marycarol Reilly

Cindy Roberts

Glynnis Rogero

Kathy Sturgis

Cindy Weaver

Janet Wenzel

Preface

"The Master of the Art of Living"—this poem helps to capture the attitudes and feelings felt in creating this cookbook. We have dedicated numerous hours collecting, cooking, and choosing the recipes you will find within *Tropical Settings*. For these efforts the cookbook committee wishes to thank our league members, families and friends. Without their help we would never have been able to create this exciting cookbook. Since 1966, the Junior League of Ft. Myers, then known as the Junior Welfare League, has been dedicated to creating a better community through voluntarism. The first 20 years of the League's existence saw the creation of the Nature Center and our first cookbook, *Gulfshore Delights*. In 1986, feeling that the Welfare League and community would benefit, the Junior Welfare League joined the Association of Junior Leagues International and changed its name to the Junior League of Ft. Myers, Inc. The League has continually striven to design, staff and fund projects that will enhance the quality of life in Southwest Florida. Recognizing the many good causes competing for corporate and private dollars, it is our goal to provide projects that are responsive to community needs while being well organized and fiscally responsible. Keeping these goals in mind we have focused in the areas of education, arts, feeding the homeless, women, children and the environment. Proceeds from the sales of *Tropical Settings* will be returned to the community through the Junior League of Ft. Myers projects. For this we thank you the consumer. Your purchase of *Tropical Settings* will allow us to meet these goals.

The Master of the Art of Living

The master of the art of living

draws no sharp distinction

between her labor and her leisure,

her mind and her body,

her work and her play,

her education and her recreation,

she hardly knows which is which.

She simply pursues her vision of excellence

through whatever she is doing,

and leaves others to determine

whether she is working or playing,

to herself, she is always doing both.

Acknowledgements

For their generous support in the making of *Tropical Settings*,
The Junior League of Ft. Myers thanks...

Publix Supermarket
The Wine Merchant
The Mill Bakery, Eatery and Brewery
The Perfect Setting
Bocilla Island Club
St. Charles Harbor
Captiva Charters
Skip One Seafood
Ron & Forrest Campbell's Garden
Ron Campbell
Paul Peden
Craig Peden
Tim Salko
Richard and Claudia Cowart
Nancy Campbell
Steve Waugh
Susan Stewart
Annette Belleau
Mrs. Erv Ibach

Photography: Greg Ross, Ross Studios
Food Stylist and Set Designer: Jan Campbell
Floral Stylist: Rhonda Shook
Floral and Landscape Design: Susan Stewart
Photographer's Assistant and Stylist: Melissa Masters

Contents

Introduction

Tropical Settings...the name evokes images of warm and gentle breezes, crystal clear waters and sandy shores. From the banks of the Caloosahatchee River to the Gulf of Mexico, southwest Floridians are surrounded by these amenities all year. Because of this you will find an emphasis on outdoor dining. Whether it be a picnic on the beach or a candlelight dinner by the pool, attitudes here are casual with a flair of southern hospitality. Our rich heritage dates back to the 1700s, when the area was inhabited by the Calusa Indians and the Barrier Islands were the home to pirates looking for refuge from the Gulf water. Through the years Ft. Myers became the winter home for Thomas Edison and Henry Ford, two men whose inventive genius has changed our world forever. It's no wonder that this beautiful area has become one of the fastest growing cities in America today. In its second cookbook, *Tropical Settings*, The Junior League of Ft. Myers brings you over 250 recipes reflecting both a tropical flavor as well as timeless classics handed down for generations. Each recipe has been tested twice and enthusiastically approved by our tasting teams to ensure that even the novice cook will be able to prepare the most elegant meal. In each photograph throughout the book we have strived to depict the casual elegance of southwest Florida living and entertaining. With fresh seafood from the local waters and fruits and vegetables from area farms and orchards, you can just add a bottle of wine, a bouquet of fresh flowers, a gentle breeze and a brilliant sunset, then sit back and enjoy the perfect tropical setting.

Appetizers

Grilled Antipasto Platter

Grilling enhances the flavor of any food, and should not be reserved just for meat and seafood. The grilled vegetables in this recipe give a boost to both the flavor and the texture and make this antipasto a little different. You may substitute grilled shrimp, scallops and crab claws for the cold cuts and garnish with lemon wedges.

For the marinade

$1/2$ cup olive oil
1 tablespoon balsamic vinegar or 2 tablespoons red wine vinegar
1 tablespoon Dijon mustard
3 cloves of garlic, minced
$1/3$ cup chopped fresh basil or $1^1/2$ teaspoons dried basil
$1/2$ teaspoon salt
$1/2$ teaspoon pepper

For the antipasto

2 eggplant   2 teaspoons salt
1 red bell pepper
1 yellow bell pepper   12 mushrooms
1 large red onion, sliced $1/2$ inch thick
2 zucchini, sliced diagonally $1/2$ inch thick
6 ounces mozzarella or provolone cheese, thinly sliced
6 ounces thinly sliced Italian cold cuts
1 tomato, cut into wedges $1/2$ cup black olives

To prepare the marinade

Combine the olive oil, vinegar, mustard, garlic, basil, salt and pepper in a bowl and whisk to mix well.

To prepare the antipasto

Cut the eggplant into $1/2$-inch slices. Sprinkle with the salt and place in a colander to drain for 30 minutes. Rinse with cold water. Spray the vegetables with olive oil. Place the bell peppers on a grill sprayed with olive oil. Grill over medium-hot coals for 15 to 20 minutes or until charred. Cool slightly. Peel and seed the peppers and cut into 1-inch wide strips. Grill the mushrooms and onions for 8 to 10 minutes, turning occasionally. Grill the eggplant and zucchini for 10 to 15 minutes or until tender but not charred. Dip the mushrooms into the marinade, turning to coat well. Arrange in a shallow dish. Repeat with the remaining vegetables, arranging separately in the dish. Drizzle with remaining marinade. Marinate in the refrigerator for 8 to 24 hours. Let stand until room temperature. Arrange with the cheese and cold cuts on a large platter. Add the tomatoes and olives.

Serves Twelve
Preparation Time: 30 minutes, plus marinating time
Cooking Time: 30 minutes

Beef Wellington Miniatures

Although the wrapping of these miniature versions of a classic favorite requires a little time, it is easy to do and the ease of serving them will more than make up for the time required in preparation.

Ingredients

1 cup dry sherry
$1/2$ cup soy sauce
4 cloves of garlic, minced
1 (3-pound) beef tenderloin
1 pound fresh mushrooms
8 ounces cream cheese
1 teaspoon Worcestershire sauce
1 teaspoon seasoning salt
1 package frozen puff pastry, thawed

Directions

Combine the wine, soy sauce and garlic in a shallow dish. Trim the beef and cut into 1-inch cubes. Add to the marinade, stirring to coat well. Marinate in the refrigerator for 8 hours or longer; drain.

Purée the mushrooms, cream cheese, Worcestershire sauce and seasoning salt in the food processor. Cut the pastry into $1/4$x2-inch strips. Arrange 2 strips at a time in an X on work surface. Place 1 beef cube in the center of each. Top with a dollop of the mushroom mixture. Fold the strips over the beef and press to seal. Arrange on a baking sheet. Bake at 425 degrees for 15 minutes.

Serves Forty-Eight
Preparation Time: 20 minutes, plus marinating time
Cooking Time: 15 minutes

Bleu Cheese and Pear Pizza

*The combination of the rye flour in the crust with the topping
of pears, Gruyère cheese and bleu cheese is delicious and different—one that
your guests have probably never tried before, but which they will look
forward to trying again. Substitute packaged pizza dough or a boboli crust
if you don't have time for the rising steps here.*

For the dough

2 teaspoons dry yeast
1 teaspoon dark brown sugar
1¹/₂ cups lukewarm water
³/₄ cup rye flour
2³/₄ cups (or more) all-purpose flour
1 tablespoon olive oil
Salt to taste

For the topping

4 (8-ounce) pears, peeled, thinly sliced
Juice of ¹/₂ lemon
2¹/₄ cups grated Gruyère cheese
1¹/₂ cups crumbled bleu cheese
¹/₄ cup melted butter

To prepare the dough

Sprinkle the yeast and brown sugar over the lukewarm water in a warm
bowl and stir to dissolve. Combine the rye flour, all-purpose flour, olive oil
and salt in a bowl and mix well. Add the yeast mixture and mix to form a
dough. Knead on a lightly floured surface for 10 minutes, kneading in
additional flour if needed. Place in a greased bowl and cover with plastic wrap.
Let rise for 45 to 60 minutes or until doubled in bulk. Punch dough down,
shape into a ball and place in greased bowl. Let rise, covered, for 30 minutes
or until doubled in bulk. Divide the dough into 3 portions. Roll each portion
into a 10- or 11-inch circle. Place each in a pizza pan sprinkled with cornmeal.

To top and bake the pizza

Rub the pear slices with lemon juice to prevent discoloration. Arrange
a layer of pear slices in a circle about 1 inch from the edge of each pizza.
Sprinkle with the Gruyère cheese. Arrange a second row of pear slices inside
the first row. Sprinkle with the bleu cheese. Brush the rim of each pizza with
melted butter. Bake at 500 degrees for 10 to 20 minutes or until the crusts
are golden brown.

Serves Twelve
Preparation Time: 30 minutes, plus rising time
Cooking Time: 10 to 20 minutes

Polenta Toast with Roasted Peppers

Polenta, a mush made from cornmeal, is a staple of northern Italy. In this recipe, it is baked until golden brown and given a colorful and flavorful update with a topping of roasted red, green and yellow peppers.

Ingredients

1/3 cup finely chopped onion
1 tablespoon olive oil
2 1/2 cups chicken broth
2/3 cup yellow cornmeal
2 tablespoons grated Parmesan cheese
1/4 teaspoon salt
1/8 teaspoon cayenne pepper
1 red bell pepper
1 green bell pepper
1 yellow bell pepper
1 tablespoon red wine vinegar
1 tablespoon chopped fresh basil
1/4 teaspoon salt

Directions

Sauté the onion in the olive oil in a 4-quart saucepan over low heat until tender. Stir in the chicken broth and cornmeal. Bring to a boil and cook for 10 minutes or until thick, stirring occasionally. Stir in the cheese, 1/4 teaspoon salt and cayenne pepper. Spread evenly in a 12x17-inch dish lined with foil. Chill for 2 hours or until firm.

Broil the bell peppers until evenly charred. Remove from the oven and place in a paper bag to cool. Remove and discard the skin and cut the peppers into strips.

Combine with vinegar, basil and 1/4 teaspoon salt in a bowl. Invert chilled polenta onto work surface and peel off foil. Cut into triangles. Arrange on baking sheet. Bake at 425 degrees for 15 minutes or until golden brown. Serve roasted peppers over polenta toast.

Serves Ten
Preparation Time: 30 minutes, plus chilling time
Cooking Time: 15 minutes

Marinated Mushrooms

Marinated mushrooms will keep for several weeks in the refrigerator and are wonderful to have on hand for parties, snacks or salads.

Ingredients

1 pound fresh mushrooms
$1/2$ cup dry vermouth
$1/2$ cup olive oil
$1/2$ cup red wine vinegar
2 tablespoons chopped onion
1 clove of garlic, crushed
$1/2$ teaspoon sugar
1 tablespoon basil
$1/2$ teaspoon dry mustard
1 teaspoon salt
$1/2$ teaspoon pepper

Directions

Cut very large mushrooms into halves or quarters. Place in a large jar. Combine the wine, olive oil, vinegar, onion, garlic, sugar, basil, dry mustard, salt and pepper in a bowl and mix well. Pour over the mushrooms and seal. Store in the refrigerator.

Serves Eight
Preparation Time: 10 minutes

Crab-Stuffed Mushrooms

The addition of just four ounces of crab meat makes these stuffed mushrooms a really elegant addition to any party. They can be prepared in advance and only need about ten minutes of baking time to be ready to serve.

Ingredients

14 large button mushrooms
2 tablespoons minced onion
1 or 2 cloves of garlic, minced
3 tablespoons olive oil
4 ounces crab meat
4 ounces fresh spinach, chopped
Tabasco sauce to taste
1/4 teaspoon Old Bay seasoning
1/8 teaspoon dried thyme
1/8 teaspoon salt
Freshly ground pepper to taste
1/4 cup milk
2 tablespoons bread crumbs
4 ounces Monterey Jack cheese, cut into 14 small thin slices

Directions

Remove the stems of the mushrooms and chop, reserving the caps. Sauté the onion and garlic in the olive oil in a skillet until tender. Add the crab meat, spinach, mushroom stems, Tabasco sauce, Old Bay seasoning, thyme, salt and pepper. Sauté until the spinach is wilted. Stir in the milk. Simmer for 4 minutes. Add the bread crumbs and mix well.

Stuff the mixture in the mushrooms and arrange in a baking dish oiled with olive oil. Top each mushroom with a slice of cheese. Bake at 350 degrees for 8 to 10 minutes or until golden brown.

Serves Fourteen
Preparation Time: 15 minutes
Cooking Time: 8 to 10 minutes

Baked Stuffed Mussels

This is a delicious and different variation of the classic, Oysters Rockefeller, using fresh mussels in place of the oysters.

Ingredients

4¹/2 pounds fresh mussels   ¹/2 cup cooked chopped spinach
¹/2 cup grated Parmesan cheese
4 cloves of garlic, chopped   1 egg
Grated rind of 1 lemon
Salt and pepper to taste
¹/2 cup fine dry bread crumbs
¹/4 cup extra-virgin olive oil

Directions

Wash mussels, discarding any that are open. Combine with water to cover in a large saucepan over medium heat. Cook just until the shells open. Remove the mussels from the shells. Place each mussel in a half shell and arrange on a baking sheet. Mix the next 5 ingredients in a bowl. Season with salt and pepper. Spoon onto the mussels and sprinkle with the bread crumbs and olive oil. Bake at 400 degrees for 10 minutes. Serve immediately.

Serves Eight
Preparation Time: 30 minutes
Cooking Time: 15 minutes

Lime-Glazed Seafood Kabobs

Grill vegetable kabobs at the same time to serve with this.

Ingredients

1 pound swordfish   1 pound large shrimp
1 pound scallops   ¹/4 cup lime juice
²/3 cup olive oil   2 to 4 tablespoons hot pepper sauce
1 teaspoon sugar   Salt and pepper to taste

Directions

Cut the swordfish into chunks. Peel the shrimp, leaving tails intact. Combine the seafood in a large shallow dish. Mix the remaining ingredients in bowl. Pour over the seafood. Marinate for 15 minutes. Thread the seafood onto skewers and return to the marinade until they go on the grill. Grill over medium heat for 4 to 6 minutes on each side or until cooked through.

Serves Twenty
Preparation Time: 15 minutes, plus marinating time
Cooking Time: 8 to 12 minutes

Oysters with Bacon and Balsamic Vinegar

The balsamic vinegar and bacon used to prepare this oyster appetizer give it a zippy and different taste that would also be good with other seafood appetizers.

Ingredients

36 fresh oysters
12 ounces bacon
1/4 cup balsamic vinegar
1/3 cup dry red wine
2 to 3 green onions, finely chopped
1 cup butter, chilled, cut into tablespoons
Salt and pepper to taste
1/4 cup balsamic vinegar

Garnish

Parsley
Lemon wedges

Directions

Arrange the oysters on half shells on a baking sheet. Cook the bacon in a skillet just until it starts to brown. Drain the bacon and cut into 1 1/2-inch pieces. Combine 1/4 cup vinegar, wine and green onions in a small skillet. Cook over medium heat until the liquid is reduced to 2 tablespoons. Reduce the heat to low. Whisk in the butter 1 tablespoon at a time; remove from the heat. Season with salt and pepper. Spoon onto the oysters and top with 1 piece of bacon. Drizzle with 1/4 cup vinegar.

Broil 6 inches from the heat source in a preheated broiler for 2 minutes. Raise the broiler rack to 2 inches from the heat source. Broil for 30 seconds or until the bacon is crisp. Spoon any cooking juices over the oysters and serve with cocktail forks. Garnish with parsley and lemon wedges.

Serves Twelve
Preparation Time: 15 minutes
Cooking Time: 2 to 3 minutes

Marinated Shrimp

*Marinated shrimp will be the most popular dish at any party
or gathering and probably the easiest to prepare. It will be even easier if
you have a seafood store that will steam the shrimp for you. The secret
with shrimp, of course, is not to overcook it.*

Ingredients

1 pound (24-count) shrimp
2 tablespoons vinegar
2 tablespoons lemon juice
$1/4$ cup vegetable oil
1 small onion, minced
2 cloves of garlic, minced
3 tablespoons horseradish
1 tablespoon minced fresh parsley
$1/4$ teaspoon paprika
1 teaspoon salt
$1/8$ teaspoon pepper

Directions

Cook the shrimp in boiling water in a saucepan for 4 minutes or just until cooked through. Rinse in cold water immediately to arrest cooking; drain in a colander.

Combine the vinegar, lemon juice, oil, onion, garlic, horseradish, parsley, paprika, salt and pepper in a bowl and mix well. Add the shrimp and stir to coat well. Marinate in the refrigerator for 4 hours or longer, stirring occasionally. Serve with cocktail picks.

Serves Eight
Preparation Time: 15 minutes, plus marinating time
Cooking Time: 4 minutes

Shark Seviche

The fresh lime juice in this dish "cooks" the shark meat. The addition of the jalapeño peppers, avocado and cilantro give it a south-of-the-border flavor, a colonial nod to its Spanish heritage.

Ingredients

1 pound fresh shark fillets
1 to 1 1/2 cups fresh lime or lemon juice
1 medium onion, thinly sliced into rings
3 jalapeño peppers, chopped   1 large avocado, chopped
1/4 cup chopped cilantro   1/4 cup olive oil
2 tablespoons white wine vinegar   Salt and pepper to taste

Directions

Cut the shark into 1/2-inch cubes. Combine with the lime juice in a medium glass bowl. Marinate in the refrigerator for 12 hours, stirring occasionally. Combine the onion, peppers, avocado, cilantro, olive oil, vinegar, salt and pepper in a bowl and mix gently. Fold into the shark mixture. Chill until serving time.

Serves Six
Preparation Time: 30 minutes, plus marinating time

Spinach and Basil Hors d'Oeuvre

This delicious low-fat spread becomes even healthier if it is served on slices of zucchini, yellow squash or peeled cucumber.

Ingredients

1/2 cup coarsely chopped fresh spinach
1 medium clove of garlic, minced   1 shallot, minced
1 teaspoon dried basil   1 cup nonfat cottage cheese
1 teaspoon (or more) olive oil
24 Melba toast rounds   1/2 red bell pepper, finely chopped

Directions

Combine the spinach, garlic, shallot and basil in a blender or food processor container and process until smooth. Add the cottage cheese and 1 teaspoon olive oil, processing constantly. Add additional olive oil only if needed for desired consistency. Chill until serving time. Spread on Melba toast rounds; top with red bell pepper.

Serves Twenty-Four
Preparation Time: 20 minutes

Baby Brie in Phyllo

The flavor of the apricot preserves makes it a perfect complement for slices of fresh apples and pears. It makes a beautiful presentation, but is so easy to do with the frozen phyllo leaves.

Ingredients

3 sheets thawed frozen phyllo dough
2 tablespoons melted butter or margarine
1 (4½-ounce) round of Brie or Camembert cheese
1 tablespoon apricot preserves

Directions

Cut the phyllo dough into halves. Place 1 sheet of phyllo dough on a work surface, leaving the remaining dough covered with a damp cloth to prevent drying out. Brush the dough with butter. Place the cheese round in the center. Spread with the preserves. Wrap the dough to enclose the cheese. Repeat the wrapping process with the remaining phyllo dough, brushing each sheet with butter and turning the cheese over after wrapping each sheet. Brush with the remaining butter. Chill, covered, in the refrigerator. Place in a shallow baking dish. Bake at 425 degrees for 8 to 12 minutes or until golden brown. Let stand for 10 minutes. Serve warm with apple and pear slices.

Serves Four
Preparation Time: 20 minutes, plus chilling time
Cooking Time: 8 to 12 minutes

Baked Brie with Pecans

The crunch of the pecans with the smooth texture of the baked brie will be a popular combination and one that is easy enough to serve for any occasion—even with very little notice.

Ingredients

1 (8-ounce) round of Brie cheese
¼ cup packed dark brown sugar
1 to 2 tablespoons brandy or whiskey   ½ cup chopped pecans

Directions

Place the cheese on an oven-proof platter. Bake at 500 degrees for 4 to 5 minutes. Combine the brown sugar, brandy and pecans in a bowl and mix well. Spread on the cheese. Bake for 2 to 3 minutes longer or until cheese is of the desired consistency.

Serves Four
Preparation Time: 10 minutes
Cooking Time: 6 to 8 minutes

Chick-Pea and Pesto Spread

The addition of the basil pesto and vegetables, particularly the zucchini, give a different twist to this dish similar to the Middle Eastern dish called hummus.

Ingredients

1 (16-ounce) can chick-peas, drained 1 cup light sour cream
3/4 cup basil pesto 1 small zucchini, shredded
1 small tomato, chopped 3/4 cup grated Parmesan cheese

Directions

Combine the chick-peas and sour cream in a food processor and process until smooth. Spoon the mixture into a mound on a serving platter. Spoon the pesto evenly over the top. Sprinkle with the shredded zucchini, tomato and cheese. Garnish with fresh basil leaves. Serve with assorted crackers or bread sticks.

Serves Sixteen
Preparation Time: 15 minutes

Garbanzo Pâté

The names garbanzo bean and chick-pea, used in the recipe above, refer to the same legume used extensively in the Middle East, India and the Mediterranean.

Ingredients

2 cups cooked garbanzos 1/2 cup chopped scallions
2 cloves of garlic, crushed 1 tablespoon Dijon mustard
Juice of 1 lemon 1 tablespoon olive oil
1/2 teaspoon crushed basil 1/2 teaspoon dill
1/2 teaspoon tarragon 1/4 teaspoon allspice
Salt and cayenne pepper to taste

Directions

Process the garbanzos, scallions, garlic, mustard, lemon juice, olive oil, basil, dill, tarragon, allspice, salt and cayenne pepper in a food processor until smooth. Add water 1 teaspoon at a time if needed for desired consistency, processing constantly. Chill for several hours. Spoon into serving dish and garnish with chopped black olives and paprika. Serve with pita triangles.

Serves Sixteen
Preparation Time: 10 minutes

Lobster Spread

If the occasion does not call for serving every guest his own lobster, treat them to this special lobster spread before the main course.

Ingredients

8 ounces cream cheese, softened
1 tablespoon milk
1 1/2 cups flaked lobster or crab meat
2 tablespoons chopped onion
1/2 teaspoon horseradish
1/4 teaspoon salt
Pepper to taste
1/4 cup sliced almonds
Paprika to taste

Directions

Blend the cream cheese and milk in a bowl. Add the lobster, onion, horseradish, salt and pepper; mix well. Spread in a greased 8-inch oven-proof dish. Sprinkle with almonds and paprika. Bake at 375 degrees for 15 minutes or until bubbly. Serve warm with crackers.

Serves Twelve
Preparation Time: 5 minutes
Cooking Time: 15 minutes

Mullet Spread

In spite of mullet's reputation as a trash fish, this tasty spread won't serve as many people as you might think and it always goes fast. It should be cool enough to hold its shape when it is served; it will be gone before it has time to get runny.

Ingredients

2 cups smoked mullet, skinned, boned
1/3 cup buttermilk
2 1/2 tablespoons lime or lemon juice
8 ounces cream cheese, softened

Directions

Combine the mullet, buttermilk and lime juice in a food processor. Process until smooth. Add the cream cheese, processing constantly until smooth. Chill, covered, for 1 hour or up to several weeks.

Serves Sixteen
Preparation Time: 10 minutes

Mushroom Spread

Florida is the third largest mushroom-producing state in the United States—a year-round and ever-growing market. Although Americans are sampling more of the exotic mushrooms, 99% of the market is still made up of the dependable white button mushroom. You can use the mushroom of your choice in this dish.

Ingredients

4 slices bacon
8 ounces mushrooms, chopped
1 medium onion, finely chopped
1 clove of garlic, minced
2 tablespoons flour
$1/4$ teaspoon salt
$1/8$ teaspoon pepper
8 ounces cream cheese, cubed
2 teaspoons Worcestershire sauce
1 teaspoon soy sauce
$1/2$ cup sour cream

Directions

Cook the bacon in a skillet until crisp. Drain and crumble the bacon, reserving 2 tablespoons drippings. Sauté the mushrooms, onion and garlic in the reserved drippings in the skillet until tender and most of the liquid has evaporated.

Stir in the flour, salt and pepper. Add the cream cheese, Worcestershire sauce and soy sauce. Heat until cream cheese melts, stirring to mix well. Stir in the sour cream and bacon. Cook just until heated through; do not boil. Spoon into a serving dish. Serve warm with crackers.

Serves Eight
Preparation Time: 10 minutes
Cooking Time: 10 minutes

Alligator Eye

This is an interesting alternative to salsa. The flavor only improves with the time it is allowed to marinate in the refrigerator.

Ingredients

2 large tomatoes, chopped
1 bunch green onions, chopped
1 (13-ounce) can chopped black olives
1 (7-ounce) can chopped green chiles
$^1/_2$ to $^3/_4$ cup medium salsa   3 tablespoons vegetable oil
2 tablespoons cider vinegar

Directions

Combine the tomatoes, green onions, black olives, green chiles, salsa, oil and vinegar in a bowl and mix well. Marinate in the refrigerator for 6 hours or longer. Serve with tortilla chips.

Serves Twenty-Four
Preparation Time: 15 minutes, plus marinating time

Aloha Shrimp Dip

The flavors of the islands give a lift to this dip featuring fresh shrimp, coconut, raisins, chutney and curry powder. It's a perfect appetizer for a "tropical setting."

Ingredients

$^1/_2$ cup sliced almonds $^1/_2$ cup shredded coconut
8 ounces cream cheese, softened
3 tablespoons sour cream $1^1/_2$ teaspoons curry powder
$^1/_2$ cup sliced green onions $^1/_2$ cup raisins
1 pound fresh shrimp, cooked, peeled, chopped
1 (8-ounce) jar mango chutney

Directions

Spread the almonds and coconut on a baking sheet. Bake at 350 degrees for 10 minutes or until lightly toasted, stirring once. Combine the cream cheese, sour cream and curry powder in a bowl and mix until smooth. Stir in the green onions, raisins and shrimp. Shape into a ball and place on a serving plate. Spoon the chutney over the top and sprinkle with the almonds and coconut.

Serves Sixteen
Preparation Time: 20 minutes
Cooking Time: 10 minutes

Tangy Tortilla Dip

This versatile mixture can also be used as a topping for fajitas.

Ingredients

1 cup nonfat sour cream
2 tablespoons orange juice
1 tablespoon Key lime juice
4 teaspoons chopped jalapeño peppers
$1/2$ teaspoon cumin

Directions

Combine the sour cream, orange juice, lime juice, peppers and cumin in a bowl and mix well. Chill for 1 hour or longer before serving. Serve with tortilla chips.

Serves Eight
Preparation Time: 10 minutes, plus chilling time

Bleu Cheese Fondue

Fondue is not just fun to eat, it is fun to do and a nice way to break the ice as your guests gather around the fondue pot. For variety, try dipping small cooked new potatoes, cornichons, celery sticks or carrot sticks.

Ingredients

16 ounces cream cheese
1 cup milk
1 teaspoon Worcestershire sauce
$1/4$ teaspoon garlic powder
8 ounces bleu cheese, crumbled

Directions

Melt the cream cheese with the milk in a saucepan over low heat, stirring to mix well. Add the Worcestershire sauce and garlic; mix well. Stir in the bleu cheese until melted. Spoon into a fondue pot to keep warm for serving. Serve with bread cubes or bite-size vegetables for dipping.

Serves Sixteen
Preparation Time: 10 minutes
Cooking Time: 10 minutes

Brunch, Breads, and Beverages

Brunch

Breads

Beverages

*Photograph Recipe
Wine: Fleur de Carneros Pinot Noir, 1992

Gratin of Fresh Fruit

You can vary the fresh fruit in this gratin to take advantage of the produce in season. It is a beautiful accompaniment to any brunch or luncheon.

Ingredients

1 medium navel orange
$^1/_2$ cup water
3 egg yolks
3 tablespoons sugar
2 tablespoons whipping cream
1 cup strawberries
1 cup sliced kiwifruit
1 cup sliced pineapple

Directions

Remove the zest in very fine strips from half the orange with a vegetable peeler. Combine the zest with the water in a small saucepan. Bring to a boil and boil for 30 seconds. Rinse under cold water and drain. Squeeze and strain the juice from the orange and measure $^1/_4$ cup plus 1 teaspoon.

Whisk the orange juice with the egg yolks, sugar and whipping cream in a double boiler. Cook over hot water until frothy and thick enough to coat a spoon, whisking constantly. Remove from the heat and stir in the orange zest; set aside to cool.

Place $^3/_4$ cup of the mixed fruit in each of four 4-inch ramekins. Spoon the custard over the fruit. Place on a baking sheet. Broil 3 inches from the heat source in preheated broiler for 30 seconds or just until light brown; do not overcook.

Serves Four
Preparation Time: 10 minutes
Cooking Time: 15 minutes

Tropical Fruit Crisp

*We think of mangos and papayas as more exotic fruits and that
is just what makes this dish exciting. They are available in most markets
year round now, however, and can bring a welcome touch of the
tropics to any meal at any time of the year.*

Ingredients

1 mango, peeled, chopped
1 papaya, peeled, chopped
3 oranges, peeled, sliced, seeded
2 tablespoons minced crystallized ginger
1 cup sugar
1 pineapple, peeled, cored, thinly sliced

Directions

Toss the mango, papaya and orange with the ginger and half the sugar
in a medium bowl. Spoon into a baking dish. Arrange the pineapple over the
top and sprinkle with the remaining sugar.

Broil under a preheated broiler for 10 minutes or until the top is crusty.
Serve immediately.

Serves Twelve
Preparation Time: 15 minutes
Cooking Time: 10 minutes

Fruit Puff

This is a fabulous accompaniment to a brunch, but it is also the perfect light dessert for other meals. You can use other fresh fruits of your choice to fill the center.

Ingredients

2 eggs
3 egg whites
$1/2$ cup skim milk
1 tablespoon vanilla extract
$1/2$ cup flour
Salt to taste
1 to 2 tablespoons fresh lemon juice
$1/2$ cup confectioners' sugar
1 cup sliced strawberries
1 cup sliced bananas
1 cup sliced peaches
1 cup raspberries

Directions

Spray a 10-inch skillet with nonstick cooking spray and place in an oven preheated to 425 degrees. Whisk the eggs, egg whites, skim milk and vanilla in a bowl until smooth. Add the flour and salt; whisk until well mixed. Pour into the heated skillet.

Bake at 425 degrees for 15 to 20 minutes or until puffed and the edges are brown and crisp. Sprinkle with half the lemon juice and confectioners' sugar. Fill the center with fruit and sprinkle with the remaining lemon juice and confectioners' sugar. Slice to serve.

Serves Six
Preparation Time: 10 minutes
Cooking Time: 15 to 20 minutes

Fresh Fruit Omelet

This version of a fresh fruit omelet calls for kiwifruit and peaches.
Other combinations which would be just as delicious include strawberries
and bananas or raspberries and blackberries. Use the
combination that best suits your taste.

Ingredients

4 eggs
$1/4$ teaspoon salt
$1/4$ cup sugar
1 cup flour
$1^1/3$ cups milk
2 tablespoons lemon juice
1 teaspoon grated lemon rind
2 apples, peeled, cut into quarters
2 tablespoons margarine
$1/2$ to 1 cup low-fat vanilla yogurt
2 to 3 cups sliced kiwifruit and peaches

Directions

Combine the eggs, salt, sugar, flour, milk, lemon juice and lemon rind in a blender container and process for several seconds or until smooth. Add the apples and pulse just until apples are coarsely chopped.

Melt the margarine in a quiche pan or pie plate in a 450-degree oven. Swirl the plate to coat evenly. Pour the batter into the plate. Bake at 450 degrees for 20 to 25 minutes or until puffed and light brown; the top will begin to crack. Top with the yogurt and fresh fruit. Serve with additional fresh fruit.

Serves Six
Preparation Time: 10 minutes
Cooking Time: 20 to 25 minutes

Cheesy Egg and Mushroom Casserole

This is an ideal way to prepare eggs for a large group. You can prepare the dish in advance and chill it until time to bake.

For the cheese sauce

2 tablespoons flour
2 tablespoons melted butter or margarine
2 cups milk
1 cup shredded Colby cheese
1/2 teaspoon salt
1/8 teaspoon pepper

For the eggs

1/4 cup chopped green onions
3 tablespoons butter or margarine
12 eggs, beaten
8 ounces fresh mushrooms, sliced
1 cup dry bread crumbs
1/8 teaspoon paprika
3 tablespoons melted butter or margarine

To prepare the cheese sauce

Blend the flour into the melted butter in a saucepan. Add the milk, cheese, salt and pepper. Cook over medium-low heat until thickened, stirring constantly. Set aside.

To prepare the eggs and bake the dish

Sauté the onion in 3 tablespoons butter in a large skillet until tender. Add the eggs. Cook until soft-set, stirring constantly. Fold in the mushrooms. Add the cheese sauce and mix gently. Spoon into a 7x12-inch baking dish. Toss the bread crumbs and paprika with 3 tablespoons melted butter in a bowl. Sprinkle over the casserole. Chill, covered, for 30 minutes or longer. Bake, uncovered, at 350 degrees for 30 minutes.

Serves Ten
Preparation Time: 30 minutes
Cooking Time: 30 minutes

Lobster and Fresh Vegetable Frittata

Nothing could be more of a treat than this version of a frittata made with lobster, but it would be just as good with other kinds of seafood— or just with the colorful fresh vegetables. The best part is that it is baked, freeing the hostess to enjoy her party, too.

Ingredients

1/2 to 3/4 medium red onion, thinly sliced
2 cloves of garlic, minced
3 small summer squash, sliced
1 yellow bell pepper, cut into thin strips
2 red bell peppers, cut into thin strips
3 tablespoons olive oil
6 eggs or 4 eggs and 2 egg whites
1/4 cup whipping cream
3 tablespoons chopped fresh basil
Salt and pepper to taste
8 ounces Boursin cheese
1 pound lobster, cooked, chopped
2 cups shredded Gruyère cheese

Directions

Sauté the onion, garlic, squash and bell peppers in the olive oil in a 2-quart saucepan for 10 minutes. Whisk the eggs and whipping cream in a bowl. Add the basil, salt and pepper. Crumble in the Boursin cheese. Stir in the lobster, sautéed vegetables and Gruyère cheese.

Pour into a buttered springform pan and place pan on a baking sheet. Bake at 350 degrees for 45 minutes or until firm. Let stand for 10 minutes. Place on a serving plate and remove the side of the pan. Cut into wedges and serve immediately.

Serves Eight
Preparation Time: 15 minutes
Cooking Time: 45 minutes

Vegetable Frittata

This is great for breakfast, for a late-night snack or a boat picnic. You can substitute Monterey Jack cheese, Cheddar cheese or your family's favorite for the Swiss cheese.

Ingredients

2 green onions, chopped
1/4 green bell pepper, chopped
4 or 5 fresh mushrooms, sliced
1 small zucchini, sliced
1 tablespoon olive oil
3 eggs
2 egg whites
2 tablespoons low-fat milk
1/4 cup shredded Swiss cheese
1/2 tomato, chopped
1/4 to 1/2 cup shredded Swiss cheese

Garnish

Chopped tomato
Chopped green onions

Directions

Sauté the green onions, green pepper, mushrooms and zucchini in the olive oil in a large skillet just until tender. Beat the eggs, egg whites and milk in a bowl. Add to the skillet and sprinkle with 1/4 cup cheese. Cook until the edges begin to brown. Sprinkle with the tomato and remaining cheese.

Broil in a preheated oven for 5 minutes or until brown and bubbly. Garnish with additional chopped tomato and green onions.

Serves Two
Preparation Time: 10 minutes
Cooking Time: 15 minutes

Herbed Eggs in Toast Baskets

Use the freshest herbs you can for this egg dish. Chives, basil, savory, oregano, parsley and tarragon all have a natural affinity for eggs.

Ingredients

4 slices whole wheat bread
2 tablespoons melted butter (optional)
5 eggs or 3 eggs and 2 egg whites
2 tablespoons milk
2 tablespoons chopped fresh herbs
2 teaspoons Creole seasoning
Salt and pepper to taste

Garnish

Chopped fresh herbs

Directions

Trim the crusts from the bread. Press gently into muffin cups sprayed with nonstick cooking spray, leaving corners to form points. Brush with butter. Bake at 400 degrees for 10 minutes; keep warm.

Beat the eggs, milk, fresh herbs, Creole seasoning, salt and pepper in a bowl. Pour into nonstick skillet. Cook until soft-set, stirring constantly. Serve in toast baskets. Garnish with additional fresh herbs.

Serves Four
Preparation Time: 10 minutes
Cooking Time: 15 minutes

Orange Oatmeal Pie

This pie is good enough to encourage your family to "eat your oatmeal" and special enough to serve to guests.

Ingredients

6 eggs, lightly beaten
1 (12-ounce) can evaporated milk
1 cup orange juice
1 cup rolled oats
1/4 cup sugar
1/4 cup melted butter
1 unbaked (9-inch) pie shell

Directions

Combine the eggs, evaporated milk, orange juice, oats, sugar and butter in a bowl and mix well. Pour into the pie shell. Bake at 375 degrees for 35 to 40 minutes or until set.

Serves Six
Preparation Time: 10 minutes
Cooking Time: 35 to 40 minutes

Veal and Spinach Pie

You can vary the proportions of this versatile pie, increasing or decreasing the veal or spinach to suit your taste. The onion can also be sautéed if you prefer.

Ingredients

1 unbaked deep-dish pie shell
1 egg white
$1/2$ to 1 pound ground veal
1 egg, at room temperature, beaten
$1/2$ cup milk
$1/2$ cup bread crumbs
1 small onion, chopped
2 teaspoons Worcestershire sauce
$1/2$ teaspoon pepper
1 (10-ounce) package frozen spinach, thawed, drained
$1^1/2$ cups shredded mozzarella cheese

Directions

Brush the pie shell with the egg white and prick with a fork. Bake at 400 degrees for 10 minutes.

Combine the veal, egg, milk, bread crumbs, onion, Worcestershire sauce and pepper and mix well. Spread in the pie shell. Top with the spinach and cheese. Bake at 350 degrees for 45 to 60 minutes or until the veal is cooked through and the crust is golden brown.

Serves Six
Preparation Time: 20 minutes
Cooking Time: 45 to 60 minutes

Individual Seafood Quiches

*These creamy easy-to-pick-up individual pies are perfect
to serve for a brunch. Just add fresh fruit and a dessert for a delightful
light meal with a tropical flair.*

Ingredients

1 recipe 2-crust pie pastry
$3/4$ cup chopped cooked shrimp
$1/4$ cup sliced green onions
1 cup shredded Swiss cheese
$1/3$ cup milk
2 eggs
$1/2$ cup mayonnaise
$1/4$ teaspoon dried dillweed
$1/4$ teaspoon salt

Directions

Divide the pastry into 2 portions and roll each into a 12-inch circle on a floured surface. Cut each into six 4-inch circles. Fit into twelve $2^{1}/_{2}$-inch muffin cups. Sprinkle shrimp, green onions and cheese into the cups.

Combine the milk, eggs, mayonnaise, dillweed and salt in a bowl and mix well. Pour over the shrimp mixture. Bake at 400 degrees for 15 to 20 minutes or until set and golden brown.

Serves Twelve
Preparation Time: 30 minutes
Cooking Time: 15 to 20 minutes

Fiesta Quiche

*Fiesta Quiche is actually low in fat and cholesterol, but not in flavor.
With it, you can plan a brunch to take advantage of the current popularity
for dishes with a southwestern flair and not even feel guilty.*

Ingredients

4 (8-inch) tortillas
$1/2$ cup shredded reduced-fat Cheddar cheese
1 (4-ounce) can chopped green chiles, drained
$1/4$ cup sliced green onions
$1/2$ cup picante sauce
1 cup egg substitute
$1/3$ cup skim milk
$1/2$ teaspoon chili powder
$1/4$ teaspoon cracked pepper
6 tomato slices
2 tablespoons nonfat plain yogurt
6 sprigs fresh cilantro

Directions

Spray a 12-inch quiche dish with nonstick cooking spray and line with
the tortillas. Sprinkle the cheese, green chiles and green onions over the tortillas
and dollop with the picante sauce.

Combine the egg substitute, skim milk, chili powder and pepper in a
bowl. Pour into the prepared dish. Bake at 350 degrees for 30 to 35 minutes
or until set. Arrange the tomato slices around the edge and top each slice with
1 teaspoon yogurt and a sprig of cilantro. Cut into wedges.

Serves Six
Preparation Time: 10 minutes
Cooking Time: 30 to 35 minutes

Fresh Tomato Tart

Fresh Tomato Tart is great for brunch, a light luncheon, or as a side dish. For variety, you may add any vegetables you like, including white or black beans.

Ingredients
1 can crescent rolls
1 to 2 tablespoons olive oil
1¹/₂ cups mozzarella, Monterey Jack or goat cheese
2 tablespoons chopped fresh basil
1 or 2 tomatoes, sliced

Directions
Unroll the dough and press into a 9-inch tart pan, trimming edge. Drizzle with half the olive oil and sprinkle with half the cheese and basil.

Arrange the tomato slices in the prepared pan. Drizzle with the remaining olive oil and sprinkle with the remaining cheese and basil. Bake at 400 degrees for 15 minutes or until golden brown. Cut into wedges to serve.

Serves Six
Preparation Time: 10 minutes
Cooking Time: 15 minutes

Tomato Quiche

The secret to this dish is the Fresh Tomato Purée on page 43.
It is the perfect dish for a summer luncheon.

Ingredients

1/4 cup shredded Swiss cheese
1/4 cup grated Parmesan cheese
1 unbaked (9-inch) pie shell
1 cup whipping cream
1/2 cup half-and-half
3 eggs
3/4 cup Fresh Tomato Purée
1/2 teaspoon salt
1/4 teaspoon white pepper

Garnish

1 tomato, sliced

Directions

Sprinkle the cheeses into the pie shell. Combine the whipping cream, half-and-half, eggs, tomato purée, salt and white pepper in a bowl and mix well. Spoon into the prepared pie shell.

Bake at 375 degrees for 45 to 50 minutes or until the quiche is set and the crust is brown. Let stand for 20 to 30 minutes before serving. Garnish with the sliced tomato.

Serves Six
Preparation Time: 10 minutes
Cooking Time: 45 to 50 minutes, plus standing time

Fresh Tomato Purée

*Make this when tomatoes are in season and freeze
it in the amounts needed for Tomato Quiche or other dishes
calling for tomato purée.*

Ingredients

3/4 cup minced onion
2 tablespoons butter
2 1/4 pounds tomatoes, peeled, seeded, chopped
1/8 teaspoon sugar
1 tablespoon minced parsley
1/2 teaspoon thyme
1 bay leaf
1/2 teaspoon salt
1/4 teaspoon pepper

Directions

Sauté the onion in the butter in a heavy skillet until tender and golden brown. Add the tomatoes, sugar, parsley, thyme, bay leaf, salt and pepper and mix well. Cook, covered, over low heat for 10 minutes.

Increase the heat and remove the cover. Cook until the liquid has evaporated and the mixture forms a thick purée. Discard the bay leaf. Cool to room temperature.

Yields Two Cups
Preparation Time: 10 minutes
Cooking Time: 20 minutes

Cheese Linzer Torte

Serve this beautiful torte with a Vouvray or Merlot for a very special brunch or luncheon. The recipe can also be made in two eight-inch pies.

Ingredients

1 (11-ounce) package pie crust mix
$1/3$ cup chopped almonds
6 ounces Swiss cheese, shredded
1 teaspoon caraway seeds (optional)
3 eggs
1 cup light cream
2 tablespoons minced onion
1 teaspoon salt
$1/4$ teaspoon pepper

Directions

Prepare the pie crust mix using package directions for double crust, adding the almonds. Roll $2/3$ of the dough into a 11x15-inch rectangle on a lightly floured surface. Place in a greased 9x13-inch baking pan. Sprinkle with the cheese and caraway seeds.

Beat the eggs with the cream, onion, salt and pepper in a bowl. Pour evenly over the cheese.

Bake at 350 degrees for 20 minutes. Roll the remaining dough into a rectangle on a floured surface and cut into $3/4$-inch strips. Arrange in a lattice over filling. Bake for 15 to 20 minutes longer or until puffed and brown.

Serves Eight
Preparation Time: 20 minutes
Cooking Time: 35 to 40 minutes

Classic Cuban Sandwich

This authentic version of the Cuban sandwich is heated in brown paper. Just be sure that the brown paper you use is not made of recycled paper, which releases toxic chemicals when heated.

Ingredients

1 loaf Cuban bread
2 tablespoons mayonnaise
2 tablespoons mustard
4 ounces thinly sliced deli baked ham
4 ounces thinly sliced deli pork
4 ounces thinly sliced salami
8 ounces thinly sliced Swiss cheese
$1/2$ large dill pickle, thinly sliced

Directions

Slice the bread into halves lengthwise. Spread 1 cut side with mayonnaise and the other with mustard. Layer the ham, pork, salami, cheese and pickle on the bottom half and replace the top. Cut into 4 pieces. Wrap in brown paper and twist ends to seal.

Bake at 350 degrees for 15 to 20 minutes or until the sandwich is heated through and the cheese is melted.

Serves Four
Preparation Time: 10 minutes
Cooking Time: 15 to 20 minutes

Baked Swiss Grits

Grits are finely ground dried corn, cooked with water to a thick porridge-like consistency and typically served with butter, salt and pepper. Native Floridians and Southerners share an appreciation for grits in many delightful variations of the basic recipe, such as these with cheese, or with garlic and other seasonings.

Ingredients

4 cups milk
$1/2$ cup butter, cut into pieces
1 cup uncooked regular grits
1 teaspoon salt
4 ounces Swiss cheese, shredded
$11/2$ ounces Parmesan cheese, grated

Directions

Bring the milk to a boil in a saucepan and stir in the butter and grits. Remove from the heat and add the salt and cheeses. Beat with an electric mixer for 5 minutes.

Spoon into a baking dish. Bake at 350 degrees for 1 hour.

Serves Eight
Preparation Time: 10 minutes
Cooking Time: 1 hour

Pine Island Popovers

Don't save this special treat for a party: wake up your family
this weekend with popovers served with confectioners' sugar, butter, jam,
honey or butter whipped with strawberries.

Ingredients

1 cup flour, sifted
3/4 teaspoon salt
1 cup cool milk
1 tablespoon vegetable oil or clarified butter
2 or 3 eggs, at room temperature

Directions

Grease popover tins and place in a 415-degree oven to heat. Mix the flour and salt in a bowl. Mix the milk and oil in a small bowl. Stir into the flour mixture. Beat in the eggs 1 at a time. Beat for 2 minutes longer.

Fill heated popover tins 3/4 full. Bake at 415 degrees for 30 to 40 minutes or until tops are deep golden brown and sides are crisp. Slit tops with knife to allow steam to escape for crisp popovers.

Serves Eight
Preparation Time: 10 minutes
Cooking Time: 30 to 40 minutes

Orange Muffins

You will think that these are magical muffins because they always disappear so quickly. Make them in miniature muffin tins for a brunch or luncheon.

Ingredients

1 cup butter, softened
1 cup sugar
2 eggs
1 teaspoon baking soda
1 cup buttermilk
2 cups flour, sifted
Grated rind of 2 oranges
1/2 cup pecans or golden raisins
1/2 cup orange juice
1 cup packed brown sugar

Directions

Cream the butter and sugar in a mixer bowl until light and fluffy. Beat in the eggs. Dissolve the baking soda in the buttermilk in a cup. Add to the creamed mixture alternately with the flour, mixing well after each addition. Stir in the orange rind and pecans.

Spoon into greased muffin cups, filling 2/3 full. Bake at 400 degrees for 20 to 25 minutes or until golden brown. Mix the orange juice and brown sugar in a bowl. Spoon over the muffins. Remove to a serving plate.

Serves Twelve
Preparation Time: 15 minutes
Cooking Time: 20 to 25 minutes

Sunshine Muffins

Laden with fruit and nuts, these muffins will bring a touch of tropical sunshine to any brunch or breakfast and really don't need any additional spread.

Ingredients

$^1/_2$ cup milk
$^1/_4$ cup vegetable oil
2 eggs
$^1/_2$ cup raisins
$1^1/_2$ cups rolled oats
2 cups baking mix
$^1/_2$ cup sugar
$^1/_2$ cup packed brown sugar
1 teaspoon cinnamon
$^1/_2$ cup shredded carrot
1 cup shredded apple
1 (12-ounce) can crushed pineapple, drained
$^1/_4$ cup chopped walnuts

Directions

Combine the milk, oil and eggs in a medium bowl and beat lightly. Stir in the raisins and oats. Let stand for several minutes. Add the baking mix, sugar, brown sugar, cinnamon, carrot, apple, pineapple and walnuts and mix just until moistened.

Spoon into greased muffin cups, filling $^1/_2$ full. Bake at 400 degrees for 20 minutes or until golden brown.

Serves Twelve
Preparation Time: 15 minutes
Cooking Time: 20 minutes

Carrot Bread

This moist bread is similar to the classic carrot cake and is good enough to serve as a dessert. Spread it with cream cheese for delicious finger sandwiches.

Ingredients

1¹/₂ cups flour
1 cup sugar
1 teaspoon baking powder
1 teaspoon baking soda
1 teaspoon cinnamon
¹/₄ teaspoon salt
¹/₂ cup vegetable oil
2 eggs, beaten
1 teaspoon vanilla extract
1 cup grated carrots
¹/₂ cup chopped pecans (optional)

Directions

Mix the flour, sugar, baking powder, baking soda, cinnamon and salt in a bowl. Add the oil, eggs and vanilla and mix well. Stir in the grated carrots and pecans.

Spoon into a greased loaf pan. Bake at 325 degrees for 1 hour. Remove to a wire rack to cool.

Serves Twelve
Preparation Time: 10 minutes
Cooking Time: 1 hour

Miniature Raspberry Loaves

Be sure to make a lot of these, because everyone will want his own miniature loaf—especially when they learn that they are lower in fat and cholesterol than most sweet breads. They also make welcome gifts.

Ingredients

2 cups flour
1 tablespoon baking powder
1 teaspoon baking soda
1/4 teaspoon salt
1/8 teaspoon cinnamon
1 cup packed light brown sugar
1/4 cup canola oil
1 cup nonfat plain yogurt
1 cup low-fat cottage cheese
1/2 cup buttermilk
1 egg
2 egg whites
Grated zest of 2 lemons
4 cups raspberries
1 cup confectioners' sugar
1/4 cup lemon juice

Directions

Sift the flour, baking powder, baking soda, salt and cinnamon into a bowl. Mix the brown sugar and oil in a medium bowl. Combine the yogurt, cottage cheese and buttermilk in a blender until smooth. Add to the brown sugar mixture. Stir in the egg, egg whites and 3/4 of the lemon zest. Stir in the flour mixture gradually. Fold in the raspberries gently.

Spoon into miniature loaf pans that have been sprayed with nonstick cooking spray and lightly floured, filling 1/2 full. Bake at 350 degrees for 50 minutes or until a wooden pick inserted in the center comes out clean. Cool in the pans on a wire rack for 20 minutes. Remove to the rack to cool completely.

Mix the confectioners' sugar, lemon juice and remaining lemon zest in a bowl. Drizzle over the loaves.

Serves Twelve
Preparation Time: 15 minutes
Cooking Time 50 minutes

Avocado Toast

*For a tropical twist to this recipe, replace the crumbled bacon
with smoked salmon. Avocados are admittedly higher in calories than other
fruits, but the fiber in them helps fight cancer and the potassium helps
lower blood pressure. Avocados also have protein, vitamins A, B complex
and E, calcium, iron, magnesium and phosphorus.*

Ingredients

4 slices rye bread
1 ripe avocado, peeled, mashed
Salt and pepper to taste
4 slices bacon, crisp-fried, crumbled (optional)

Directions

Toast the bread in a toaster oven or under the broiler for 3 to 5 minutes
or until light brown. Spread with the mashed avocado and sprinkle with salt
and pepper. Sprinkle with the bacon and slice diagonally.

Serves Four
Preparation Time: 10 minutes
Cooking Time: 3 to 5 minutes

Bleu Bread

*Bleu Bread is a quick trick made with Italian bread and bleu cheese salad
dressing that is sure to please both the hurried hostess and her guests.*

Ingredients

1 loaf Italian bread, sliced
1/2 cup margarine, softened
Garlic powder to taste
1/2 (16-ounce jar) bleu cheese salad dressing
1/4 to 1/2 cup grated Parmesan cheese

Directions

Spread the bread slices with the margarine and arrange on a baking sheet.
Sprinkle with garlic powder. Bake at 400 degrees for 5 to 7 minutes or until
heated through. Spread with the salad dressing and sprinkle with the cheese.
Broil for 3 to 5 minutes or until bubbly. Serve immediately.

Serves Twelve
Preparation Time: 10 minutes
Cooking Time: 8 to 12 minutes

Herbed Biscuits

Just allow thirty minutes for the herbs to flavor the butter for this easy bread made with canned refrigerator biscuits.

Ingredients

1/4 cup butter or margarine
1 1/2 teaspoons chopped fresh parsley
1/2 teaspoon dillweed
1 teaspoon minced onion
2 teaspoons grated Parmesan cheese
1 (10-count) can buttermilk biscuits

Directions

Melt the butter in a saucepan. Stir in the parsley, dillweed, onion and cheese. Let stand for 30 minutes. Cut each biscuit into halves horizontally and arrange 1 inch apart in a baking pan. Brush on all sides with the butter mixture. Bake for 12 to 15 minutes or until golden brown.

Serves Ten
Preparation Time: 5 minutes, plus marinating time
Cooking Time: 12 to 15 minutes

Savory Bread

Savory Bread leftovers make wonderful croutons for salads and soups, but since guests usually make quick work of it, you may have to double the recipe if you expect to have any left.

Ingredients

1/4 cup butter
3 tablespoons Salad Supreme seasoning
3 tablespoons Worcestershire sauce
1 loaf French bread

Directions

Microwave the butter in a glass dish until melted. Stir in the Salad Supreme seasoning and Worcestershire sauce. Slice the bread horizontally and place on a baking sheet. Brush with the butter mixture. Broil for 2 to 3 minutes or until bubbly. Serve warm.

Serves Twelve
Preparation Time: 5 minutes
Cooking Time: 2 to 3 minutes

Chocolate Biscotti

*Your mother told you never to dip your bread in your coffee
or milk, but she wasn't referring to these crisp biscotti, which are
designed for just that purpose—so enjoy!*

Ingredients

2 eggs
2 egg whites
1 teaspoon vanilla extract
$1/2$ teaspoon almond extract
$1^1/4$ cups sugar
2 cups flour
$1/3$ cup baking cocoa
2 tablespoons instant espresso
1 teaspoon baking soda
Salt to taste
$1/2$ cup sliced almonds
12 ounces bittersweet chocolate

Directions

Combine the eggs, egg whites and flavorings in a mixer bowl and beat
until smooth. Add the sugar, flour, baking cocoa, espresso granules, baking
soda and salt and mix to form a dough. Mix in the almonds. Knead several
times on a lightly floured surface with floured hands and a spatula. Shape into
2 rolls, 15 inches in length and 2 inches in diameter. Place on a baking sheet
with sides not touching.

Bake at 325 degrees for 40 minutes. Cool for 10 minutes. Reduce the
oven temperature to 275 degrees. Cut the rolls diagonally into $3/4$-inch slices.
Arrange the slices on a baking sheet sprayed with vegetable oil. Bake for 20
to 24 minutes, turning after 10 to 12 minutes. Turn off the heat and let stand
in closed oven for 15 minutes. Remove to a wire rack to cool completely.

Melt the chocolate in a saucepan over low heat. Dip each cookie halfway
in the chocolate. Place on waxed paper until firm. Store in an airtight container.

Serves Thirty-Two
Preparation Time: 30 minutes
Cooking Time: $1^1/2$ hours

Almond Iced Tea

This is wonderful to serve for special occasions, or just to keep in the refrigerator. It is actually better the second day, but you will have to plan ahead, or it won't last that long.

Ingredients

5 tablespoons unsweetened instant tea
2 cups water
1^1/$_2$ cups sugar
2 cups water
1 (12-ounce) can frozen lemonade, thawed
1 tablespoon vanilla extract
1 tablespoon almond extract
2 quarts water

Directions

Dissolve the instant tea in 2 cups water in large container. Combine the sugar with 2 cups water in a small saucepan. Simmer until the sugar dissolves. Add to the instant tea mixture with the lemonade, flavorings and 2 quarts water; mix well. Chill for 8 hours or longer. Serve over ice.

Serves Twelve
Preparation Time: 15 minutes
Cooking Time: 5 minutes

Morning Coffee Cooler

Make just one recipe of this to enjoy on a hot morning, or increase it by as much as you need to serve a crowd.

Ingredients

1 cup strong coffee
^{1}/$_4$ cup nonfat plain yogurt
^{1}/$_2$ cup skim milk
Sugar to taste
^{1}/$_4$ cup ice cubes

Directions

Process the coffee and yogurt in a blender until smooth. Add the skim milk, sugar and ice cubes and process until the ice is processed to the desired consistency. Strain if desired and serve immediately.

Serves One
Preparation Time: 5 minutes

Coffee Punch

Surprise your guests with this delicious version of their morning eye-opener. It does double duty at a brunch as dessert and coffee. For variety, use one of the new flavored coffees.

Ingredients

1 gallon cold coffee
$1/2$ gallon light cream
1 quart milk
1 gallon vanilla ice cream, chopped
2 cups whipped cream
2 cups shaved chocolate
$3 1/2$ tablespoons cinnamon

Directions

Freeze half the coffee in ice cube trays. Combine the ice cubes with the remaining coffee, cream, milk and ice cream in a punch bowl and mix gently. Let stand for 30 minutes before serving. Top with the whipped cream, chocolate shavings and cinnamon. Serve in punch cups. You may add sugar to taste if desired.

Serves Fifty
Preparation Time: 10 minutes, plus freezing time and standing time

Berry Pineapple Shake

Share this touch of the tropics with a friend and make any morning special. You can substitute fresh fruits in season for the ones here.

Ingredients

1 cup fresh strawberry halves
1 cup fresh pineapple chunks
$1/2$ cup fresh raspberries
2 tablespoons thawed apple juice concentrate
8 to 10 ice cubes

Directions

Combine the strawberries, pineapple, raspberries, apple juice concentrate and ice cubes in a blender and process until smooth. Serve immediately.

Serves Two
Preparation Time: 5 minutes

Fresh Citrus Cooler

To make the sugar water for this cooler, dissolve 1 cup sugar in 1/2 cup water in a saucepan over low heat. Cool it to room temperature and chill until serving time.

Ingredients

1 cup fresh orange juice   3/4 cup fresh grapefruit juice
1/4 cup fresh lime juice   1/4 cup fresh lemon juice
1/2 cup sugar water   1/4 cup club soda   1/2 cup ice cubes

Garnish

Citrus slices

Directions

Combine the orange juice, grapefruit juice, lime juice, lemon juice and sugar water in a pitcher. Stir in the club soda and ice cubes at serving time. Garnish with citrus slices.

Serves Two
Preparation Time: 10 minutes

Kiwifruit Float

The kiwifruit originated in New Zealand and takes its name from the flightless bird. Actually, it looks more like a hairy egg and has a sweet-tart flavor unlike any other fruit. It is also delicious in salads, desserts or as a colorful garnish.

Ingredients

2 kiwifruit, peeled, sliced   1 (12-ounce) can piña colada mix
1 banana, sliced   3 drops of green food coloring (optional)
8 scoops vanilla ice cream
2 (12-ounce) cans ginger ale, chilled
Nutmeg to taste

Directions

Combine the kiwifruit, piña colada mix, banana and food coloring in a blender or food processor container and process for 1 to 2 minutes or until smooth. Pour into a covered 1-quart pitcher and place in the freezer for 1 hour. Pour about 1/4 cup into each of eight 6-ounce glasses and add a scoop of ice cream. Fill the glasses with the ginger ale and sprinkle with the nutmeg. Stir gently with an up and down motion and serve immediately.

Serves Eight
Preparation Time: 10 minutes, plus freezing time

Minty Lemon-Lime Freeze

Enjoy this tropical treat year round. The fresh mint leaves are essential, but they are available in most well-stocked supermarkets now at any time of the year.

Ingredients

1 banana
6 mint leaves
$1/2$ cup orange juice
Grated zest of 1 lime
1 cup skim milk
$1/4$ cup ice cubes

Directions

Purée the banana in a blender. Add the mint leaves, orange juice, lime zest, skim milk and ice cubes and process until slushy. Serve immediately.

Serves Two
Preparation Time: 5 minutes

Southwest Florida Sunrise Shake

If you like a more tart flavor, squeeze the juice of half a lemon into the blender before mixing.

Ingredients

1 pint fresh strawberries
2 medium bananas
$1/2$ cup orange juice
6 to 8 ice cubes

Garnish

Strawberries or orange slices

Directions

Combine the strawberries, bananas and orange juice in a blender container and process until the fruit is coarsely chopped. Add the ice cubes and process until smooth. Pour into tall glasses. Garnish with a strawberry or orange slice.

Serves Two
Preparation Time: 5 minutes

Bloody Mary Mix

*Let this mix age for 48 hours or longer to blend the flavors. Add
a celery stalk stirrer for color and crunch.*

Ingredients

1 (46-ounce) can tomato juice
1¹/₂ ounces lemon juice
³/₄ ounce Worcestershire sauce
1 teaspoon dillweed
¹/₂ teaspoon garlic salt
1 teaspoon celery salt
¹/₄ teaspoon pepper

Directions

Combine the tomato juice, lemon juice, Worcestershire sauce, dillweed,
garlic salt, celery salt and pepper in a covered container. Chill for 48 hours
before serving.

Serves Six
Preparation Time: 5 minutes, plus aging time

Peach Fuzzies

*Serve tall frosty glasses of Peach Fuzzies as part of a brunch
buffet and you will get things off to a great start—even with people
who think they don't like fruity drinks.*

Ingredients

1 (8-ounce) can sliced peaches
1 (6-ounce) can frozen pink lemonade
6 ounces vodka
6 to 8 ice cubes
1 ounce peach brandy
1 teaspoon sugar

Directions

Drain the peaches, reserving ¹/₄ cup juice. Process the lemonade and
vodka in a blender just until mixed. Add the ice cubes and process until
smooth. Add the peaches, reserved juice, brandy and sugar and process until
smooth. Serve in chilled glasses.

Serves Four
Preparation Time: 10 minutes

Sangria Blanca

*The Spanish word sangria means bleeding and inspires the name
for the drink, which is typically red. This version bleeds white, however,
and is made with white wine and green or white fruits. In either
version, it is a welcome cooler for a hot day.*

Ingredients

1 (750-milliliter) bottle dry white wine
1 large pear, peeled, thinly sliced
2 kiwifruit, peeled, sliced   1 cup seedless green grapes
1 orange, thinly sliced   3 tablespoons sugar
2 tablespoons Cognac   3 tablespoons Cointreau
1¹/₂ cups sparkling water

Garnish

Mint sprigs or orange wedges

Directions

Combine the wine, pear, kiwifruit, grapes, orange, sugar, Cognac and
Cointreau in a large glass pitcher. Chill, covered, for 4 hours or longer. Add
the sparkling water at serving time and mix gently. Serve over ice in tall glasses.
Garnish with sprigs of mint or orange wedges.

Serves Six
Preparation Time: 10 minutes, plus chilling time

Turquoise Margaritas

*The turquoise color of this cooling drink comes from the blue
Curaçao, which is available in most liquor stores.*

Ingredients

6 lime slices   Coarse salt to taste
1¹/₂ cups Margarita mix   ³/₄ cup tequila
¹/₄ cup blue Curaçao   ¹/₂ lime, cut into quarters   4 cups ice

Directions

Rub 1 lime slice around the rim of each of 6 glasses and reserve the lime
slices. Dip the rims into salt. Combine the Margarita mix, tequila, blue
Curaçao and lime quarters in a blender and process until the lime is finely
chopped. Add the ice and process until smooth. Pour into the prepared glasses
and garnish with the reserved lime slices.

Serves Six
Preparation Time: 5 minutes

Soups and Salads

Photograph Recipes

Asparagus Soup

Have you ever wondered why some asparagus is thin and some is plump? The reason is that the male stalks are lean, and the female stalks are plump. Why doesn't that surprise anyone? It is also useful to know that the lean stalks are no more tender than the plump ones.

Ingredients

2^1/2 pounds fresh asparagus
1 cup Chardonnay or dry white wine
1 teaspoon dried tarragon
^{1}/2 teaspoon salt
^{1}/4 teaspoon pepper
^{1}/4 cup butter or margarine
5 tablespoons flour
3^1/2 cups chicken broth
2 cups half-and-half
1 teaspoon dried tarragon

Directions

Trim about 1 inch from the ends of the asparagus. Steam the stalks until tender and drain. Process in a food processor or blender until smooth and set aside.

Bring the wine, 1 teaspoon tarragon, salt and pepper to a boil in a small saucepan. Reduce the heat and simmer for 20 minutes. Strain and set aside.

Melt the butter in a large heavy saucepan and stir in the flour until smooth. Cook over medium heat for 1 minute, stirring constantly. Whisk in the chicken broth gradually. Cook until thickened, stirring constantly. Add the wine mixture, asparagus purée, half-and-half and 1 teaspoon tarragon. Bring just to a boil and reduce heat. Simmer for 20 minutes.

Serves Eight
Preparation Time: 10 minutes
Cooking Time: 1 hour

Collard Green and Bean Soup

*Long a staple of Southern soul food, collard is a variety of
cabbage that doesn't form a head, but grows in a loose rosette at the
top of a tall stem. The greens can be prepared in any manner suitable for
cabbage or spinach. It is a good source of calcium and iron.*

Ingredients

1 (3-pound) boneless picnic ham
8 cups boiling water
2 pounds hot Italian sausage
1 tablespoon ground fennel
1 teaspoon crushed red pepper
1 (8-ounce) strip of lean bacon
2 medium onions, chopped
4 cloves of garlic, chopped
2 pounds dried Great Northern beans
3 (10-ounce) packages frozen chopped collards, thawed, drained

Directions

Trim the fat from the ham and cut into 1-inch cubes. Simmer, covered,
in the boiling water for 2 hours. Reserve the ham and cooking water. Remove
the sausage from the casings and combine with the fennel and crushed red
pepper. Shape into 1/2-inch balls. Fry in a skillet over low heat until brown.
Remove the sausage balls with a slotted spoon and drain the skillet.

Remove the fat from the bacon and cut the lean into small cubes. Fry
in the skillet until brown. Drain all but 2 tablespoons of the drippings from
the skillet. Add the onions and garlic and sauté lightly.

Bring the beans to a boil in a large saucepan and boil for 10 minutes.
Let stand for 30 minutes; drain and rinse. Add to the undrained ham with
the sausage, bacon and sautéed vegetables. Simmer, covered, until the beans
are tender-crisp. Add the collard greens. Bring to a simmer and remove from
the heat. Serve with salad and corn bread. You may freeze this soup and reheat,
stirring frequently.

Serves Sixteen
Preparation Time: 1 hour
Cooking Time: 5 hours

Curried Cauliflower and Potato Soup

We tend to think that reducing the fat in a recipe reduces the flavor, but the curry powder and ginger in this low-fat soup give it a delicious savor.

Ingredients

3 cups chopped cauliflower
1 large red potato, peeled, cut into quarters
Salt to taste
1 small onion, chopped
1 tablespoon butter
$1/2$ teaspoon ground ginger
$1/2$ teaspoon curry powder
$3/4$ cup evaporated skim milk
$11/4$ cups fat-free chicken broth
$1/4$ teaspoon salt
$1/8$ teaspoon white pepper

Directions

Combine the cauliflower and potato with lightly salted water to cover in a medium saucepan. Cook, covered, for 5 minutes. Remove 1 cup of the cauliflower and set aside. Cook the remaining vegetables until very tender. Drain and set aside.

Sauté the onion in the butter in a saucepan over medium heat for 5 minutes or until tender. Add the ginger and curry powder and cook for 30 seconds to bring out the flavor. Combine with the potato mixture and evaporated milk in a blender and process until smooth, adding some of the chicken broth if needed. Return to the saucepan with the reserved cauliflower and remaining chicken broth. Cook until heated through, but do not boil. Season with $1/4$ teaspoon salt and white pepper.

Serves Four
Preparation Time: 30 minutes
Cooking Time: 25 minutes

Gazpacho

This refreshing summertime soup, which originated in the Andalusia region of Spain, can be a meal in itself, particularly when served with additional fresh vegetables. Chopped hard-cooked eggs are also a popular garnish.

Ingredients

1/2 onion, chopped
1 clove of garlic
1 large cucumber, peeled, cut into chunks
5 or 6 large tomatoes, peeled, cut into chunks
1/2 cup torn watercress
3 tablespoons olive oil
3 tablespoons red wine vinegar
1 (12-ounce) can mixed vegetable juice cocktail
Salt to taste
8 drops of Tabasco sauce

Garnish

Chopped vegetables
Croutons

Directions

Process the onion and garlic in a food processor until smooth. Add the cucumber and tomatoes and process until coarsely chopped. Add the watercress and process briefly. Pour into a large bowl.

Whisk in the olive oil, vinegar, vegetable juice and salt. Chill until serving time. Whisk to mix well before serving. Add the Tabasco sauce. Garnish with additional chopped vegetables and croutons.

Serves Eight
Preparation Time: 30 minutes, plus chilling time

White Gazpacho

This is a new twist on the old favorite. It is wonderful to take along on a picnic or patio party in a thermos. Just chop the vegetable garnish to take along.

Ingredients

1 large onion, sliced
4 cloves of garlic, minced
3 tablespoons butter or margarine
2 cups milk
2 teaspoons instant chicken bouillon
2 teaspoons lemon juice
1 cup plain yogurt
Red pepper sauce to taste
1/2 teaspoon salt
1/8 teaspoon pepper

Garnish

Chopped fresh vegetables
Chopped hard-cooked eggs

Directions

Sauté the onion and garlic in the butter in a medium saucepan until tender. Reduce the heat to medium-low and simmer for 15 minutes. Stir in the milk and bouillon. Cook over medium-high heat until the bouillon dissolves, stirring constantly. Add the lemon juice, yogurt, pepper sauce, salt and pepper.

Process in a blender or food processor until smooth. Chill, covered, for 2 hours or up to 2 days. Garnish with chopped vegetables and/or chopped hard-cooked eggs.

Serves Four
Preparation Time: 15 minutes, plus chilling time
Cooking Time: 20 minutes

Golden Pepper and Tomato Soup

*Red and yellow bell peppers contain nearly four times as much
vitamin C as citrus oranges, more potassium than a banana and as
much fiber as a bowl of bran flakes. Besides that, they are delicious,
with this soup as a good example.*

4 yellow bell peppers
3 pints yellow cherry or pear tomatoes
1/2 cup fresh lemon juice
1/2 teaspoon sugar
1 teaspoon ground ginger
1/2 teaspoon ground anise
1/2 teaspoon freshly ground pepper
1/2 cup whipping cream
Salt to taste

Directions

Cut the peppers into 1/4-inch strips. Cut the tomatoes into halves.
Combine the peppers, tomatoes, lemon juice, sugar, ginger, anise and pepper
in a medium saucepan.

Simmer, covered, for 50 minutes, stirring occasionally. Process the
mixture in batches in a food processor. Press through a fine sieve into a bowl,
discarding the seeds and pulp. Stir in the cream and salt. Chill, covered, for
4 hours or longer.

Serves Six
Preparation Time: 15 minutes, plus chilling time
Cooking Time: 50 minutes

Cream of Peanut Soup

Peanut soup is a traditional soup of the old South, using a traditional crop of both the old and new South—peanuts. This version is quick and easy to make.

Ingredients

2 tablespoons (heaping) creamy peanut butter
1 cup hot water
1 teaspoon cornstarch
1 cup chicken stock, chilled
2 cups evaporated milk or half-and-half
2 teaspoons minced onion or onion flakes
1 teaspoon salt

Directions

Dissolve the peanut butter in the hot water in a saucepan. Blend the cornstarch into the chicken stock in a cup. Stir into the peanut butter mixture. Add evaporated milk, onion and salt.

Cook for 5 minutes or until thickened and heated through, stirring constantly. Serve hot. You may chill this soup and reheat with good results.

Serves Four
Preparation Time: 5 minutes
Cooking Time: 10 minutes

Roquefort and Spinach Soup

There is nothing wrong with the soup that just "happens" when you clean out the refrigerator and combine all the leftovers. But this is a showcase soup, using some of the most elegant ingredients that ever graced a soup bowl, and is worthy of a premier place in your recipe collection.

Ingredients

1 medium onion
2 tablespoons unsalted butter
2 tablespoons brandy
2 cups chicken stock
3 ounces Roquefort cheese, crumbled
2 cups fresh spinach, julienned
2 plum tomatoes, seeded, chopped
1 teaspoon fresh thyme or $1/4$ teaspoon dried thyme
1 tablespoon unsalted butter
6 tablespoons whipping cream
Freshly ground pepper to taste
2 tablespoons unsalted butter

Garnish

Crumbled Roquefort cheese

Directions

Cut the onion into halves and cut into thin slices. Sauté in 2 tablespoons butter in a large saucepan over low heat until golden brown. Remove the saucepan from the heat. Add the brandy and ignite; allow flames to subside. Add the chicken stock and cheese. Bring to a boil, stirring frequently. Reduce the heat to low and simmer until the cheese melts, stirring to mix well. Cool slightly.

Process the mixture in several batches in a blender or food processor. Return to the saucepan. Sauté the spinach, tomatoes and thyme in 1 tablespoon butter in a medium saucepan over medium heat for 2 minutes or until the spinach is wilted. Add to the soup with the cream. Bring to a simmer over medium heat. Season with the pepper. Stir in 2 tablespoons butter. Serve immediately. Garnish with additional cheese.

Serves Four
Preparation Time: 10 minutes
Cooking Time: 15 minutes

Cold Squash Soup

*This makes a beautiful presentation served in wine glasses
and garnished with fresh chives.*

Ingredients

2 medium white onions, chopped
1/4 cup butter
5 to 8 small to medium yellow squash, sliced
1 1/2 cups chicken stock
1/2 cup dry white wine
1/4 teaspoon sugar
1 1/2 cups whipping cream
Salt and pepper to taste

Garnish

Fresh chives

Directions

Sauté the onions in the butter in a saucepan until tender. Add the squash, chicken stock, wine and sugar. Cook for 15 to 20 minutes or until the squash is tender. Cool to room temperature.

Process the mixture in the blender until smooth. Combine with the whipping cream, salt and pepper in a bowl and mix well. Chill in the refrigerator for 4 hours or longer.

Serves Eight
Preparation Time: 10 minutes, plus chilling time
Cooking Time: 20 to 25 minutes

Wild Rice Soup

Wild rice is actually not a rice at all, but a long grain marsh grass native to the northern Great Lakes region, where it is harvested by native Americans. It is admittedly expensive, and this is a good way to enjoy its nutty flavor and chewy texture.

Ingredients

1 medium onion, minced
2 tablespoons butter
1/4 cup flour
3 1/2 cups chicken broth
2 cups cooked wild rice
1/2 cup white wine
1/3 cup minced ham (optional)
1/3 cup grated carrots
1/2 teaspoon salt
1 cup half-and-half

Directions

Sauté the onion in the butter in a saucepan until tender. Stir in the flour. Add the broth, mixing well. Cook until thickened, stirring constantly.

Add the rice, wine, ham, carrots and salt. Stir in the half-and-half. Cook over medium heat until heated through.

Serves Six
Preparation Time: 10 minutes
Cooking Time: 20 minutes

Cioppino

This is a terrific base recipe to prepare in advance and chill or freeze to take along on a fishing trip. The base is ready for the catch of the day. Just in case there is no catch of the day, keep a can of shrimp and crab stocked on board and no one will be disappointed.

Ingredients

1$1/2$ cups chopped onions
$1/2$ cup chopped parsley
1 cup chopped celery
1 cup sliced carrots
$1/2$ cup chopped green bell pepper
3 cloves of garlic, minced
$1/2$ cup olive oil
1 (29-ounce) can Italian tomatoes
1 (8-ounce) can tomato sauce
1 cup dry sherry or white wine
$1/2$ teaspoon basil
$1/2$ teaspoon fennel seeds
1 teaspoon salt
$1/4$ teaspoon pepper
2 to 2$1/2$ pounds whitefish and shellfish, such as crab, lobster, scallops and shrimp

Directions

Sauté the onions, parsley, celery, carrots, green pepper and garlic in the olive oil in a large saucepan. Add the tomatoes, tomato sauce, wine, basil, fennel seeds, salt and pepper. Simmer for 30 minutes.

Add the fish and shellfish. Simmer over low heat for 20 minutes or just until cooked through.

Serves Six
Preparation Time: 30 minutes
Cooking Time: 50 minutes

Seafood Black Bean Gumbo

Capture the flavor of the islands with this gumbo, which is even better if it is prepared a day in advance and reheated. Serve it over Spanish yellow rice, garnished with sour cream, chopped tomatoes, green onions and salsa.

Ingredients

2 cups chopped Spanish onions
2 teaspoons butter
1 cup chopped celery
1 cup chopped red bell pepper
1 teaspoon cumin
1 teaspoon thyme
1 teaspoon chopped parsley
1 teaspoon oregano
$1/2$ teaspoon Old Bay seasoning
$1/2$ teaspoon salt
1 teaspoon cracked pepper
2 tablespoons flour
1 quart fish stock or clam stock, heated
1 (16-ounce) can crushed tomatoes
$11/2$ cups cooked black beans
$11/2$ pounds fresh white fish, trimmed, chopped
$11/2$ to 2 pounds peeled shrimp, deveined
2 tablespoons Colo Lopez

Directions

Sauté the onions in the butter in a large heavy saucepan until tender. Add the celery and bell pepper. Sauté until tender. Add the cumin, thyme, parsley, oregano, Old Bay seasoning, salt and pepper. Cook for 5 minutes longer. Stir in the flour and cook until smooth.

Add the fish stock and tomatoes. Cook until slightly thickened, stirring constantly. Stir in the black beans, fish, shrimp and Colo Lopez. Simmer for 20 minutes, stirring occasionally. Adjust the seasonings.

Serves Ten
Preparation Time: 30 minutes
Cooking Time: 35 minutes

Shrimp and Andouille Sausage Gumbo

Traditional Louisiana gumbo is made with andouille sausage, as it is here.
If you can't find andouille, substitute kielbasa, and enjoy.

Ingredients

1 pound smoked andouille or kielbasa sausage
1/2 cup vegetable oil
1/2 cup flour
4 stalks celery, coarsely chopped
2 medium onions, coarsely chopped
3 medium green bell peppers, chopped
2 bay leaves
2 teaspoons oregano, crumbled
2 teaspoons salt
Cayenne pepper to taste
5 (8-ounce) bottles clam juice
1 (28-ounce) can plum tomatoes, drained, chopped
8 ounces okra, sliced 1/4 inch thick
2 pounds uncooked medium shrimp, peeled, deveined

Directions

Cut the sausage into halves lengthwise and slice 1/4 inch thick. Heat the oil in a heavy saucepan over high heat until nearly smoking. Stir in the flour. Cook for 5 to 8 minutes or until dark brown, stirring constantly.

Add the celery, onions and green peppers. Cook for 5 minutes, stirring constantly and scraping the bottom of the pan. Stir in the bay leaves, oregano, salt and cayenne pepper. Add the clam juice, tomatoes and sausage. Cook for 15 minutes. Add the okra and reduce the heat. Simmer for 15 minutes or until the okra is tender.

Chill, covered, until time to serve. Bring gumbo to a simmer over low heat. Add the shrimp. Cook for 3 minutes or just until the shrimp is tender. Remove the bay leaves. Serve over rice in large bowls.

Serves Six
Preparation Time: 15 minutes, plus chilling time
Cooking Time: 45 minutes

Avocado and Raspberry Salad

The buttery flavor of the green avocado and the tart taste of the red raspberries make this a treat for the taste buds as well as the eyes.

Ingredients

2 avocados
1 cup fresh raspberries
2 tablespoons sugar

Directions

Peel the avocado, discarding the seed. Cut each half into slices, cutting to but not through the end and fan out on 2 serving plates. Combine the raspberries and sugar in a small bowl. Spoon over the avocado fans.

Serves Four
Preparation Time: 5 minutes

Frosty Summer Fruit Salad

This is a cool summer treat that is sure to be popular with family as well as guests. Garnish it with frosted frozen grapes.

Ingredients

2 cups water
2 cups sugar
Juice and pulp of 12 juice oranges
$^1/_2$ to 1 teaspoon lemon juice and pulp
5 bananas, chopped
1 (20-ounce) can unsweetened crushed pineapple
1 (8-ounce) jar maraschino cherries, drained, chopped

Directions

Bring the water and sugar to a boil in a saucepan and boil for 10 minutes, stirring to dissolve the sugar completely. Cool to room temperature. Combine the orange juice and pulp, lemon juice and pulp, bananas, pineapple and cherries in a bowl. Add the sugar water and mix well. Spoon into a freezer container. Freeze for 1 hour or longer. Serve immediately or let stand until slushy if preferred. Serve in dessert glasses.

Serves Twelve
Preparation Time: 20 minutes, plus freezing time

Honeydew Gin Salad

There are people who think that there is a "gin season." If there is, it surely coincides with the melon season, and this salad is a delightful way to enjoy both.

Ingredients

1 honeydew melon, chilled
2 tablespoons fresh lime juice
2 tablespoons gin
2 tablespoons finely chopped fresh mint
Grated zest of 1 lime

Garnish

4 lime wedges
4 sprigs of mint

Directions

Cut the honey dew melon into quarters, discarding the seeds. Place the quarters on 4 serving plates.

Combine the lime juice, gin, chopped mint and lime zest in a bowl. Sprinkle on the melon. Garnish with lime wedges and sprigs of fresh mint. Serve immediately.

Serves Four
Preparation Time: 10 minutes

Melon and Mango Salad

*To easily prepare a mango, slice down the sides lengthwise close
to the pit. Cut each side in a checkerboard. Push up the skin side of the
mango and the squares will pop up for easy removal.*

For the dressing

$1/2$ cup fresh lemon juice
2 teaspoons sugar
1 tablespoon chopped fresh mint
$1/2$ teaspoon pepper
$1/4$ cup vegetable oil

For the salad

1 ($1^1/2$-pound) cantaloupe
1 honeydew melon
2 mangos
3 tablespoons fresh lemon juice
2 tablespoons sugar
2 tablespoons chopped fresh mint
Salt to taste
Leaves of 8 ounces fresh flatleaf parsley
$1/3$ cup salted dry-roasted sunflower seeds

To prepare the dressing

Whisk together the lemon juice, sugar, mint and pepper in a small bowl.
Whisk in the oil and set aside.

To prepare and present the salad

Cut the cantaloupe, honeydew melon and mangos into $1/2$-inch pieces.
Combine with the lemon juice, sugar, mint and salt in a bowl; mix gently.
Add half the dressing and mix gently.

Stir the parsley into the remaining dressing. Spoon the parsley mixture
around the edge of a shallow serving platter and sprinkle with the sunflower
seeds. Spoon the melon mixture into the center of the platter.

Serves Eight
Preparation Time: 15 minutes

Beef Salad

*Even the men in the crowd won't mind a salad for lunch
or supper if it includes marinated grilled beef. For variety, substitute
turkey or shrimp for the beef.*

For the marinade and beef

$1/2$ cup soy sauce
6 tablespoons sugar
1 tablespoon finely grated ginger
1 tablespoon minced garlic
1 pound flank steak or other beef

For the salad

$1/4$ cup soy sauce
2 tablespoons fresh lemon juice
2 tablespoons peanut oil
8 cups torn lettuce or other greens
$1/2$ cup sliced cucumber
$1 1/3$ cups thinly sliced red onion
1 teaspoon sesame seeds

To prepare the marinade and beef

Combine the soy sauce, sugar, ginger and garlic in a shallow dish and
mix well. Add the beef, turning to coat well. Marinate, covered, for 2 hours,
turning occasionally; drain. Grill for 10 to 20 minutes or until done to taste.
Cut cross grain into thin slices.

To prepare and present the salad

Combine the soy sauce and lemon juice in a bowl. Whisk in the peanut
oil. Combine with the lettuce, cucumber and onion in a bowl and toss lightly.
Arrange the beef over the top and sprinkle with the sesame seeds.

Serves Four
Preparation Time: 15 minutes, plus marinating time
Cooking Time: 10 to 20 minutes

Dijon Asparagus and Chicken Pasta Salad

This is especially good in the spring when tender fresh asparagus is plentiful, but it can be enjoyed year round with frozen asparagus. Substitute other pasta shapes for variety.

For the dressing

1 cup mayonnaise
2 tablespoons Dijon mustard
2 tablespoons lemon juice
1 teaspoon salt
1/2 teaspoon pepper

For the salad

6 ounces uncooked spiral pasta
10 ounces fresh asparagus or thawed frozen asparagus
1 pound boneless skinless chicken breasts, cooked
1 red bell pepper

To prepare the dressing

Combine the mayonnaise, mustard, lemon juice, salt and pepper in a bowl and mix well.

To prepare the salad

Cook the pasta *al dente* using the package directions. Rinse in cold water and drain. Steam the fresh asparagus for 3 to 4 minutes or until tender. Cool and cut into 1-inch pieces.

Cut the chicken into bite-sized pieces. Cut the bell pepper into 1/2-inch pieces. Combine the pasta, asparagus, chicken and red bell pepper in a bowl. Add the dressing and toss lightly. Chill, covered, until serving time.

Serves Six
Preparation Time: 30 minutes

Chinese Chicken Salad

Toast the almonds for this salad in an ungreased skillet on top of the stove or in a shallow baking pan in a 375-degree oven for 10 minutes.

For the dressing

1/2 cup white vinegar
1/2 cup sugar
2 1/2 teaspoons salt
3/4 teaspoon pepper
1 tablespoon sesame oil

For the salad

3 boneless skinless chicken breasts, cooked, shredded
1/4 cup toasted slivered almonds
1 head romaine lettuce, shredded
3 to 5 green onion tops, chopped
1 to 2 tablespoons chopped cilantro
1/2 cup blanched julienned carrots
1/2 cup blanched snow peas
1 tablespoon sesame seeds

To prepare the dressing

Combine the vinegar, sugar, salt and pepper in a small saucepan. Heat until the sugar dissolves, stirring constantly. Cool slightly. Stir in the oil.

To prepare the salad

Combine the chicken, toasted almonds, lettuce, green onions, cilantro, carrots, snow peas and sesame seeds in a salad bowl. Add the warm dressing and toss lightly. Serve immediately.

Serves Six
Preparation Time: 10 minutes
Cooking Time: 10 minutes

Curried Chicken Salad

Make enough chicken salad for a party with this recipe. The mango chutney and curry powder give it an exotic and tropical twist.

Ingredients

5 pounds chicken breasts, skinned, boned
1 1/2 pounds fresh broccoli
2 cups chopped scallions
2 (8-ounce) jars mango chutney
1/2 teaspoon lemon juice
3 tablespoons curry powder
2 teaspoons tarragon
2 cups mayonnaise

Directions

Rinse the chicken well. Cook in water to cover in a saucepan until tender. Drain, cool and cut into small pieces. Blanch the broccoli and drain.

Combine the chicken, broccoli and scallions in a bowl. Cut the chutney into small pieces. Combine with the lemon juice, curry powder and tarragon in a small bowl. Add to the chicken mixture and toss to mix well.

Chill until serving time. Add the mayonnaise and toss lightly. Serve in a lettuce-lined serving bowl.

Serves Fifteen
Preparation Time: 20 minutes
Cooking Time: 20 minutes

Grilled Chicken Salad with Citrus Salsa

This is also good rolled in flour tortillas or served with warmed flour tortillas for a light and satisfying summer meal.

For the salsa

1 small pink grapefruit
1 navel orange
Grated zest of 1/2 orange
Grated zest of 1/2 lime
4 scallions, thinly sliced
10 yellow and/or red cherry tomatoes, seeded, chopped
1 tablespoon fresh lime juice
1 tablespoon olive oil
1 jalapeño pepper, chopped
1/4 cup chopped cilantro
4 tomatillos, chopped (optional)
1 ounce tequila
Salt and pepper to taste

For the chicken

1/4 cup fresh lime juice
1/4 cup olive oil
1 jalapeño pepper, thinly sliced
4 boneless skinless chicken breasts, trimmed
Salt and pepper to taste
1 ounce tequila
8 cups torn fresh greens

To prepare the salsa

Peel and section the grapefruit and orange. Cut the sections into 1/4-inch pieces. Combine with the orange zest, lime zest, scallions, tomatoes, lime juice, olive oil, jalapeño pepper, cilantro, tomatillos, tequila, salt and pepper in a bowl and mix well.

To prepare the chicken and present the salad

Combine the lime juice, olive oil and jalapeño pepper in a shallow bowl. Rinse the chicken and pat dry. Rub with salt and pepper. Add to the lime juice mixture with the tequila. Marinate in the refrigerator for 30 minutes or longer; drain. Grill the chicken for 5 to 10 minutes on each side or until cooked through. Let stand for 5 minutes. Cut into thin slices. Place the greens on 4 serving plates. Arrange the chicken over the greens. Spoon the salsa over the top. Serve immediately.

Serves Four
Preparation Time: 30 minutes, plus marinating time
Cooking Time: 20 minutes

Crab Meat and Mango Salad

A mango is good when it has a smooth skin that has begun to color and has a fresh smell. Avoid buying any mangos that are bright green, very firm, discolored or bruised. The flavor of a mango is best when it is served cold.

Ingredients

1 medium onion, finely chopped
2 stalks celery, chopped
1 pound fresh crab meat, cooked
Salt and pepper to taste
$1/2$ cup vegetable oil
$1/3$ cup cider vinegar
$1/2$ cup ice water
2 or 3 mangos
2 or 3 avocados
2 tablespoons fresh lime or lemon juice

Directions

Alternate layers of the onion, celery and crab meat in a deep dish, sprinkling with salt and pepper. Combine the oil, vinegar and ice water in a bowl and mix well. Pour over the layers. Marinate in the refrigerator for 24 hours.

Peel the avocados and mangos and slice into $1/2$-inch wedges. Dip the slices into the lime juice. Arrange on 6 serving plates. Drain the crab meat mixture and spoon over the fruit wedges. Serve with additional lime wedges to squeeze over the top.

Serves Six
Preparation Time: 20 minutes, plus marinating time

Lobster Coleslaw with Fresh Herbs

Ask your fish market for female lobsters in order to take advantage of the roe. When the lobsters are cooked, retrieve the bright red roe from the area between the body and the head and push through a strainer to separate the eggs. These will add a mild sea flavor and a touch of color.

Ingredients

2 (1½-pound) lobsters
1 white onion, cut into halves and thinly sliced
1 cup mayonnaise
2 to 3 teaspoons Dijon mustard
1 tablespoon fresh lemon juice
¼ cup chopped fresh basil
3 tablespoons chopped fresh chives
1 tablespoon chopped fresh tarragon
7 cups shredded green cabbage
Salt and pepper to taste

Directions

Steam or boil the lobsters in a large pot for 10 minutes or until completely red. Drain and let stand until cool enough to handle. Twist to separate the head from the body, discarding the heads. Collect the roe and push through a strainer to separate the eggs. Remove the meat from the tails and slice thickly. Cover and set aside.

Combine the onion, mayonnaise, mustard, lemon juice, basil, chives and tarragon in a bowl. Stir in the cabbage, lobster, roe, salt and pepper. Serve immediately or chill for up to 3 hours.

Serves Eight
Preparation Time: 15 minutes
Cooking Time: 10 minutes

Shrimp and Endive Salad with Tomato Dressing

The dressing for this salad is good on many other salads and keeps well in the refrigerator. Remember to store Belgian endive wrapped in a paper towel in a plastic bag because it becomes bitter when exposed to light and has been carefully grown in the absence of light.

For the dressing

12 ounces plum tomatoes, coarsely chopped
$1/2$ cup olive oil
5 tablespoons balsamic vinegar
1 clove of garlic
Salt and pepper to taste

For the salad

4 heads Belgian endive
2 tablespoons olive oil
Salt and pepper to taste
12 shrimp, cooked, peeled, deveined

Garnish

Chopped basil

To prepare the dressing

Combine the tomatoes, olive oil, vinegar and garlic in the blender and process until smooth. Combine with salt and pepper to taste in a bowl. Chill until serving time.

To prepare the salad

Cut the endive lengthwise into thin slices. Toss with the olive oil in a large bowl. Season with salt and pepper. Spoon the dressing onto 4 serving plates. Mound the endive in the center. Arrange the shrimp around the endive and garnish with basil.

Serves Four
Preparation Time: 30 minutes

Roasted Pepper and Pasta Salad

*The red, yellow, orange and purple bell peppers which are
becoming plentiful in the markets have a wonderful flavor which
reaches its peak with roasting.*

For the dressing

1/4 cup olive oil
1 tablespoon red wine vinegar
1 tablespoon Dijon mustard
2 tablespoons chopped fresh basil
Salt and pepper to taste

For the salad

8 ounces uncooked penne
1 medium red bell pepper
1 medium yellow bell pepper
1 clove of garlic, crushed
1 medium zucchini, thinly sliced
1 tablespoon olive oil
1 tablespoon finely shredded basil

To prepare the dressing

Whisk the olive oil, vinegar, mustard, basil, salt and pepper in a bowl.
Set aside.

To prepare the salad

Cook the pasta using package directions and drain. Broil the peppers
until black blisters appear. Place in a plastic bag and let steam for 10 minutes.
Peel off the skin and cut the peppers into 1/2-inch strips. Combine with the
pasta in a large bowl.

Sauté the garlic and zucchini in the heated olive oil in a skillet over
medium heat for 3 or 4 minutes. Stir into the pasta mixture. Add the dressing
and toss to mix well. Sprinkle with the shredded basil. Chill until serving time.

Serves Four
Preparation Time: 20 minutes
Cooking Time: 10 minutes

Asparagus Salad

To serve this salad at a buffet or luncheon, arrange the marinated stalks into bundles and tie the bundles with a chive stem or green onion top.

Ingredients

2 pounds fresh asparagus
$1/4$ cup water
$1/4$ cup olive oil
1 tablespoon red or white wine vinegar
$1/4$ teaspoon garlic powder
Salt and freshly ground pepper to taste

Garnish

Lemon wedges

Directions

Combine the asparagus and water in a shallow microwave-safe dish. Microwave on High for 3 to 4 minutes. Drain and cool.

Combine the olive oil, vinegar, garlic powder, salt and pepper in a bowl. Pour over the asparagus in a shallow serving dish. Serve at room temperature. Garnish with lemon wedges.

Serves Six
Preparation Time: 10 minutes
Cooking Time: 3 to 4 minutes

Romaine and Orange Salad

This is easy to prepare and festive enough for a party—when you might want to substitute the sections of fresh oranges for the canned oranges.

For the dressing

1/2 cup mayonnaise
5 tablespoons red wine vinegar
2 tablespoons sugar
1/2 teaspoon salt

For the salad

1 bunch romaine lettuce, shredded
1 (11-ounce) can mandarin oranges, drained
1 small red onion, thinly sliced into rings
1/2 cup chopped walnuts
1/4 cup crumbled bleu cheese

Garnish

Orange wedges

To prepare the dressing

Combine the mayonnaise, vinegar, sugar and salt in a bowl; mix well.

To prepare the salad

Combine the lettuce, oranges, onion, walnuts and bleu cheese in a salad bowl. Add the dressing and toss lightly to coat well. Garnish with the orange wedges.

Serves Six
Preparation Time: 15 minutes

Black-Eyed Pea Salad

A new twist for a traditional Southern favorite: your grandmother wouldn't recognize it, but she might ask you for the recipe!

For the dressing

1/3 cup red wine vinegar
1 1/2 tablespoons country-style Dijon mustard
2 1/2 teaspoons sugar
1 cup olive oil
1 1/2 cloves of garlic, minced
1 3/4 teaspoons salt
3/4 teaspoon pepper

For the salad

3 (10-ounce) packages frozen black-eyed peas
2 medium red bell peppers, chopped
1/3 cup (scant) chopped cilantro
4 bunches arugula

Garnish

1 cup thinly sliced red onion
1 tablespoon chopped cilantro

To prepare the dressing

Whisk the vinegar, mustard and sugar in a medium bowl until the sugar dissolves. Whisk in the oil gradually. Add garlic, salt and pepper. Chill, covered, for up to 2 days.

To prepare the salad

Cook the black-eyed peas using the package directions; drain. Combine with the bell peppers and cilantro in a large bowl. Add 1 cup of the dressing and toss to coat well. Marinate in the refrigerator for 2 hours or longer. Combine the arugula with the remaining dressing in a bowl and toss lightly. Spoon onto a large serving platter. Spoon the black-eyed pea mixture into the center. Garnish with the onion and additional cilantro. You may substitute 12 ounces of dried black-eyed peas or fresh peas for the frozen peas or dandelion or mustard greens for the arugula in this recipe.

Serves Six
Preparation Time: 15 minutes, plus marinating time

Broiled Pepper Salad

*This is the perfect accompaniment for a pasta main dish: you might just stir
the leftovers together on the second day for a pasta and pepper salad.*

For the dressing

1 tablespoon olive oil
1 tablespoon tarragon vinegar
1 tablespoon lemon juice
2 cloves of garlic, crushed
1 shallot, chopped
2 teaspoons chopped fresh parsley
1 teaspoon chopped fresh tarragon
Salt and pepper to taste

For the salad

1 yellow bell pepper
1 red bell pepper
1 green bell pepper
1 teaspoon olive oil
Salt and pepper to taste

To prepare the dressing

Combine the olive oil, vinegar, lemon juice, garlic, shallot, parsley,
tarragon, salt and pepper in a small bowl and whisk to mix well. Set aside.

To prepare the salad

Cut the bell peppers into halves and arrange cut side down in a baking
dish. Sprinkle with the olive oil and sprinkle with salt and pepper. Broil on
middle oven rack for 10 to 15 minutes or until tender. Pour dressing over
peppers. Marinate in the refrigerator until serving time.

Serves Three
Preparation Time: 10 minutes, plus marinating time
Cooking Time: 10 to 15 minutes

Chick-Pea and Parsley Salad

Parsley is much more than a garnish in Middle Eastern cooking.
This combines parsley with another Middle Eastern
favorite—chick-peas—for a salad with a satisfying crunch.

Ingredients

$1/2$ cup dried chick-peas
1 cup finely chopped parsley
$1/2$ cup finely chopped onion
$1/4$ cup olive oil
$1/4$ cup lemon juice
1 small clove of garlic, crushed (optional)
$1/2$ teaspoon salt

Directions

Soak the chick-peas in water to cover in a saucepan for 8 hours or longer. Cook in the soaking water for 1 to $1\,1/4$ hours or until chick-peas are tender. Drain, reserving $1/4$ cup liquid. Combine the chick-peas with the parsley and onion in a serving bowl.

Combine the reserved liquid with the olive oil, lemon juice, garlic and salt in a bowl and mix well. Add to the salad and toss lightly to mix well. Chill until serving time.

Serves Four
Preparation Time: 20 minutes, plus soaking time
Cooking Time: 1 to $1\,1/4$ hours

Fresh Tomatoes with Basil Buttermilk Dressing

The glorious weather in southwest Florida produces an abundance of tomatoes, strawberries and citrus fruits throughout most of the year and a favorite pastime is picking your own vegetables and fruits. This recipe takes advantage of those vine-ripened tomatoes.

Ingredients

2 cups fresh basil
3/4 cup buttermilk
2 green onions, thinly sliced
3/4 teaspoon salt
3/4 cup light mayonnaise
Pepper to taste
5 or 6 vine-ripened beefsteak tomatoes

Garnish

Basil

Directions

Combine the basil, buttermilk, green onions and salt in a food processor and process until smooth. Combine with the mayonnaise and pepper in a bowl and whisk until well mixed. Let stand for 30 minutes. Chill, covered, for up to 8 hours.

Slice the tomatoes and arrange on a serving plate. Spoon the dressing over the top. Garnish with fresh basil.

Serves Eight
Preparation Time: 10 minutes, plus standing and chilling time

Marinated Tomatoes

A vine-ripened tomato is so good that it needs very little dressing up.
The beauty of this recipe is that the dressing can be prepared in advance
and the tomatoes can be marinated until needed.

Ingredients

3 large tomatoes
1/3 cup olive oil
1/4 cup red wine vinegar
1/2 clove of garlic, crushed
1 tablespoon chopped fresh basil
2 tablespoons chopped onion
1/2 teaspoon salt
1/4 teaspoon pepper

Directions

Cut the tomatoes into 1/2-inch slices and arrange in a shallow dish.
Combine the olive oil, vinegar, garlic, basil, onion, salt and pepper in a covered
jar and shake to mix well. Spoon over the tomatoes. Marinate, covered, in the
refrigerator for several hours.

Serves Six
Preparation Time: 10 minutes, plus marinating time

Yogurt Tahini Dressing

Serve this dressing over greens and garnish with toasted sesame seeds, or for
variety, serve it over meat or fish. It is also an excellent dip and makes a
beautiful presentation served in a hollowed-out cabbage.

Ingredients

1 large clove of garlic, crushed
1/2 teaspoon salt
2 cups plain yogurt
1 to 2 tablespoons tahini
Fresh lemon juice to taste

Directions

Stir the garlic and salt into the yogurt in a bowl. Add the tahini and
lemon juice and mix well. Chill until serving time.

Serves Twelve
Preparation Time: 5 minutes

Side Dishes

Vegetables

Side Dishes

*Photograph Recipes
Wine: Murphy–Goode Reserve Fume Blanc, 1993

Black Bean and Corn Salsa

Serve this salsa of black beans and corn as a cold side dish
or salad with grilled chicken or fish. If you prefer, you can substitute
Italian parsley and a clove of garlic for the cilantro.

Ingredients

2 (15-ounce) cans black beans, drained, rinsed
1 (15-ounce) can whole kernel corn, drained
1 red bell pepper, finely chopped
1 stalk celery, thinly sliced
4 scallion bulbs, thinly sliced
1/4 cup chopped cilantro
Juice of 3 limes
Hot sauce to taste
1/2 teaspoon salt

Directions

Combine the black beans, corn, bell pepper, celery, scallions, cilantro, lime juice, hot sauce and salt in a bowl and mix well. Marinate in the refrigerator for 1 hour to several days.

Serves Six
Preparation Time: 10 minutes, plus marinating time

Green Bean Bundles

*These are so easy to serve for a luncheon or buffet and can
be prepared in advance, ready to bake just before serving. The bacon and
brown sugar give them a distinctive flavor.*

Ingredients

2 pounds fresh green beans
6 slices bacon, partially cooked, cut into halves
3 tablespoons light brown sugar
Garlic salt to taste
1/4 cup melted butter

Directions

Steam the green beans until tender-crisp. Arrange in bundles of 6 to 10 beans and wrap each with 1/2 piece of bacon. Place in a baking dish. Sprinkle with the brown sugar and garlic salt and drizzle with the butter.

Bake at 350 degrees for 15 to 20 minutes or until the bacon is crisp.

Serves Six
Preparation Time: 20 minutes
Cooking Time: 15 to 20 minutes

Green Beans Caesar

The olive oil, lemon juice and Parmesan cheese in this dish give the green beans a flavor reminiscent of the famous Caesar salad. The recipe suggests serving them warm, but they would be just as good marinated in the refrigerator to serve as a salad.

Ingredients

1 1/2 pounds fresh green beans
2 cloves of garlic, minced
2 tablespoons olive oil
2 tablespoons butter
3 tablespoons fresh lemon juice
1/2 cup freshly grated Parmesan cheese
1 teaspoon coarsely ground pepper

Directions

Blanch the green beans in boiling water in a large saucepan for 3 minutes or until tender-crisp; drain.

Sauté the garlic in the heated olive oil and butter in a large skillet over medium heat for 1 minute. Stir in the lemon juice. Add the beans and stir to coat well. Sprinkle with the cheese and pepper.

Serves Six
Preparation Time: 10 minutes
Cooking Time: 10 minutes

Calico Beans

Calico beans are a good substitute for traditional baked beans that depend on bacon for flavor and can be high in fat. They are great with barbecued chicken or taken along on a picnic or tailgate party.

Ingredients

1 (16-ounce) can lima beans
1 (16-ounce) can pinto beans
1 (16-ounce) can vegetarian baked beans
1 (16-ounce) can kidney beans
1/2 cup (or more) packed brown sugar
1/2 cup reduced-sodium catsup
1/2 cup chopped onion
1 teaspoon vinegar
1 tablespoon mustard
2 slices lean Canadian bacon, trimmed, chopped

Directions

Drain the beans and combine with the brown sugar, catsup, onion, vinegar, mustard and Canadian bacon in a bowl and mix well.

Spoon into a 9x13-inch baking dish. Bake at 350 degrees for 1 1/2 hours.

Serves Twelve
Preparation Time: 10 minutes
Cooking Time: 1 1/2 hours

Broccoli in Orange-Shallot Butter

Broccoli is a perennial favorite, but everyone welcomes a new way to prepare it. Floridians like almost everything, including broccoli, with a touch of fresh orange juice and you will, too.

Ingredients

Florets of 3 pounds broccoli
Salt to taste
1/2 cup fresh orange juice
1/3 cup minced shallot
1 tablespoon grated orange rind
3/4 cup unsalted butter

Directions

Cook the broccoli in salted water to cover in a large saucepan for 5 minutes or until tender-crisp. Plunge into cold water, drain well and pat dry.

Simmer the orange juice in a small heavy saucepan for 10 minutes or until reduced to 2 tablespoons.

Combine the shallot and orange rind with the butter in a large heavy skillet. Cook, covered, over low heat for 10 minutes or until the shallots are tender, stirring occasionally. Stir in the orange juice, salt and broccoli. Increase the heat to medium and cook for 3 minutes or until heated through, stirring to coat well. Serve immediately.

Serves Six
Preparation Time: 10 minutes
Cooking Time: 25 to 30 minutes

Broccoli Sauté

*The crunch of water chestnuts along with the soy sauce, honey
and sesame seeds give this dish a delightful flavor of the Far East. It is
delicious served with grilled ribs.*

Ingredients

Florets of 1 large head broccoli
1 (8-ounce) can sliced water chestnuts, drained
1 onion, sliced
1 clove of garlic, minced
2 tablespoons reduced-sodium soy sauce
1 tablespoon honey
1 teaspoon sesame seeds

Directions

Sauté the broccoli, water chestnuts, onion and garlic in a skillet sprayed
with nonstick cooking spray for 5 minutes or until tender.

Mix the soy sauce and honey in a small bowl. Pour over the vegetables.
Cook until the flavors blend. Spoon into a serving dish and sprinkle with the
sesame seeds.

Serves Four
Preparation Time: 5 minutes
Cooking Time: 10 minutes

Sautéed Brussels Sprout Leaves

You won't have to bribe the family to eat their Brussels sprouts when you prepare them this way, but they are special enough to serve to guests as well.

Ingredients

1 pint Brussels sprouts
$1/2$ teaspoon dried thyme
Salt and pepper to taste
1 tablespoon olive oil
1 tablespoon unsalted butter
1 tablespoon chopped fresh Italian parsley
2 tablespoons chopped pistachios

Directions

Peel away the leaves from the Brussels sprouts, discarding the cores. Combine with the thyme, salt and pepper in the heated olive oil and butter in a sauté pan. Sauté over medium heat for 15 minutes or until wilted, stirring frequently. Sprinkle with the parsley and pistachios. Serve immediately.

Serves Four
Preparation Time: 10 minutes
Cooking Time: 15 minutes

Gingered Carrots

Carrots are one of the few vegetables that are even better for you cooked than uncooked. The cooking partially dissolves the cellulose-stiffened cell walls, making the nutrients more readily available.

Ingredients

6 medium carrots, scraped, sliced
2 tablespoons butter or margarine
$1^1/2$ teaspoons minced candied ginger or $3/4$ teaspoon ground ginger
1 tablespoon toasted sesame seeds
Chopped parsley to taste

Directions

Cook the carrots in water in a saucepan until tender; drain. Add the butter and ginger. Cook until glazed, stirring frequently. Sprinkle with the sesame seeds and parsley.

Serves Six
Preparation Time: 10 minutes
Cooking Time: 25 minutes

Mustard-Glazed Carrots

*Select the younger, slenderest carrots at the market to assure
their sweetness. Cut off the leaves before storing them in a plastic bag,
because the greenery robs the carrots of moisture.*

Ingredients

2 pounds carrots, scraped, sliced
1/4 cup butter or margarine
1/4 cup brown sugar mustard
1/4 cup chopped fresh parsley
Salt to taste

Directions

Cook the carrots in water in a saucepan until tender; drain. Melt the
butter in a saucepan. Add the mustard, parsley and salt. Cook for 3 minutes,
stirring constantly. Add the carrots and toss to coat well.

Serves Six
Preparation Time: 5 minutes
Cooking Time: 20 minutes

Sweet Carrot Soufflé

*Serve this soufflé as an easy alternative to sweet potatoes with
turkey, chicken, ham or pork.*

Ingredients

2 cups sliced carrots, cooked
3 eggs
2 tablespoons flour
1/2 cup sugar
1 cup milk
1/4 cup butter or margarine
1/4 teaspoon cinnamon

Directions

Combine the carrots, eggs, flour, sugar, milk, butter and cinnamon in
a blender and process until smooth. Spoon into a 9x13-inch baking dish. Bake
at 350 degrees for 45 minutes or until set.

Serves Six
Preparation Time: 10 minutes
Cooking Time: 45 minutes

Chayote in Parsley Butter

Chayote come to us from south of the border and are sometimes referred to as vegetable pears. They are actually a bland member of the squash family and can be served in the same ways.

Ingredients

4 chayote
Salt to taste
2 tablespoons butter
2 tablespoons minced fresh parsley
Pepper to taste

Directions

Cook the chayote in salted water in a saucepan for 20 minutes or until tender when pierced with a knife; drain and peel. Cut each into halves, discarding the seed, and slice into thin wedges.

Arrange the wedges on a serving platter. Melt the butter in a small heavy skillet and stir in the parsley. Drizzle over the chayote and sprinkle with salt and pepper.

Serves Eight
Preparation Time: 10 minutes
Cooking Time: 20 minutes

Leeks au Gratin

Roman legions brought the leek to Wales, where it became the national emblem. A Welsh prince instructed his soldiers to wear leeks in their caps for indentification during a battle, and loyal Welshmen still celebrate that victory with leeks on March 1, St. David's Day.

Ingredients

8 to 12 leeks, trimmed
Salt to taste
2 tablespoons flour
2 tablespoons melted butter
1 cup milk
1 cup shredded Cheddar cheese
$1/2$ teaspoon prepared mustard
$1^1/2$ teaspoons lemon juice
Pepper to taste
$1/4$ cup bread crumbs
1 tablespoon butter

Directions

Cook the leeks in salted water in a saucepan just until tender and drain. Place in a buttered baking dish.

Blend the flour into 2 tablespoons melted butter in a saucepan. Cook until smooth. Add the milk. Cook until thickened, stirring constantly. Stir in the cheese until melted. Add the mustard, lemon juice, salt and pepper and mix well. Pour over the leeks.

Sprinkle with the bread crumbs and dot with 1 tablespoon butter. Bake at 375 degrees for 25 minutes or until crisp and brown.

Serves Ten
Preparation Time: 10 minutes
Cooking Time: 35 minutes

Baked Leeks

Leeks are related to both onions and garlic, although the flavor is milder and more subtle than either. The smaller the leek, the more tender it will be. You should slit leeks from top to bottom to more easily wash away the dirt trapped between the leaf layers.

Ingredients

8 leeks
2 cups water
1 tablespoon lemon juice
Salt and pepper to taste
2 cups milk
2$^1/_2$ tablespoons flour
2 tablespoons melted butter
$^1/_3$ cup grated Gruyère cheese
$^1/_4$ teaspoon nutmeg
Paprika to taste

Directions

Cut the leeks into quarters lengthwise, leaving 1 inch at the bottom intact and rinse well. Combine with the water, lemon juice and salt to taste in a saucepan. Cook over medium heat for 16 minutes. Drain and place in a buttered baking dish. Sprinkle with salt and pepper.

Bring the milk just to a simmer in a saucepan. Blend the flour into the melted butter in a saucepan. Cook for 2 minutes over low heat, stirring constantly. Stir in the hot milk gradually and season with salt and pepper. Cook for 10 minutes or until thickened, stirring frequently.

Pour over the leeks and sprinkle with the cheese, nutmeg and paprika. Bake at 350 degrees for 20 minutes. Serve warm.

Serves Four
Preparation Time: 10 minutes
Cooking Time: 35 to 40 minutes

Mushrooms Provençale

This could also be served as an appetizer from a chafing dish.

Ingredients

2 tablespoons butter
1 teaspoon vegetable oil
1 pound mushrooms, sliced 1/4 inch thick
Salt and pepper to taste
1 tablespoon chopped chives
1 teaspoon chopped fresh parsley
2 cloves of garlic, crushed
Juice of 1/4 lemon

Directions

Heat the butter and oil in a skillet. Add the mushrooms and sprinkle with salt and pepper. Sauté for 3 to 4 minutes over medium-high heat, stirring occasionally.

Add the chives, parsley, garlic and lemon juice and mix well. Cook for 2 minutes longer and adjust the seasoning.

Serves Four
Preparation Time: 5 minutes
Cooking Time: 5 to 10 minutes

Red Wine Mushrooms

*Mashed potatoes become a company special when served with
Red Wine Mushrooms spooned over the top. The dish can be prepared
in advance and reheated at serving time.*

Ingredients

1 pound fresh large mushrooms, cut into quarters
$1/2$ cup red wine
$1/2$ cup chicken stock
1 tablespoon (about) soy sauce
$1^1/2$ teaspoons butter or margarine
Salt and freshly ground pepper to taste

Directions

Combine the mushrooms, wine, chicken stock and soy sauce in a large heavy noncorrosive skillet. Cook and stir over low heat, adding the butter in small pieces, for 10 minutes or until the mushrooms are tender and most of the liquid is absorbed. Season with salt and pepper.

Serves Six
Preparation Time: 5 to 7 minutes
Cooking Time: 15 minutes

Mushrooms and Peppers

The Dijon mustard and Worcestershire sauce give this mushroom dish
a zesty taste. It is especially good over rice.

Ingredients

1 medium onion, chopped
1/2 cup butter
1 pound mushrooms, sliced
2 green bell peppers, cut into 1-inch pieces
2 tablespoons Dijon mustard
2 tablespoons Worcestershire sauce
1/2 cup packed dark brown sugar
3/4 cup red wine
Pepper to taste

Directions

Sauté the onion in the butter in a skillet. Add the mushrooms and green pepper. Blend the mustard, Worcestershire sauce, brown sugar, wine and pepper in a small bowl. Add to the mushroom mixture. Simmer for 45 minutes. Serve over rice.

Serves Eight
Preparation Time: 5 minutes
Cooking Time: 50 minutes

Vidalia Onion Casserole

Vidalia onions are named for the town in Georgia, where they flourish in the sandy soil. They are prized in the South for their sweet dispositions and are enjoyed primarily in May and June, although advances in storage facilities have made them available during a longer period.

Ingredients

$^1/_2$ cup uncooked rice
5 cups boiling water
7 medium Vidalia onions, sliced
$^1/_4$ cup unsalted butter
1 cup shredded Swiss cheese
$^2/_3$ cup half-and-half

Garnish

Paprika

Directions

Cook the rice in the boiling water in a saucepan for 5 minutes; drain. Sauté the onions in the butter in a skillet until tender. Stir in the rice, cheese and half-and-half.

Spoon into a greased shallow baking dish. Bake at 325 degrees for 1 hour. Garnish with paprika.

Serves Six
Preparation Time: 10 minutes
Cooking Time: 1$^1/_4$ hours

Herbed Potato Wheel

*Since we eat more potatoes than any other vegetable in the United States—
more than twice as many as the tomato, which is our next
most popular vegetable—you will welcome this tasty new way to
prepare everyone's favorite.*

Ingredients

4 Idaho potatoes
1^1/$_2$ teaspoons fresh rosemary
1 to 2 teaspoons chopped Italian parsley
^{3}/$_4$ teaspoon dried thyme
Salt and pepper to taste
^{1}/$_2$ cup butter or margarine, chopped

Directions

Slice the potatoes into a bowl of cold water; drain and pat dry. Mix the
rosemary, parsley, thyme, salt and pepper in a small bowl. Arrange ^{1}/$_3$ of the
potatoes in an overlapping spiral starting in the center of a heavy nonstick
skillet. Dot with ^{1}/$_3$ of the butter and sprinkle with ^{1}/$_3$ of the herb mixture.
Repeat with the remaining ingredients.

Cook over medium heat for 30 to 40 minutes or until the bottom is
crisp and golden brown. Invert onto a flat plate and return to the skillet. Cook
for 10 to 15 minutes longer or until golden brown on the other side. Cut into
wedges to serve.

Serves Six
Preparation Time: 10 minutes
Cooking Time: 1 hour

Roasted Garlic Mashed Potatoes

We in the United States have only recently discovered what Europeans have known for years: that garlic should be enjoyed in larger quantities as a vegetable and not only as a scant flavoring.

Ingredients

2 bulbs of garlic
1 teaspoon olive oil
2 pounds potatoes, peeled
Salt to taste
2 tablespoons unsalted butter
2 tablespoons olive oil
$1/4$ to $1/2$ cup half-and-half or milk, heated

Directions

Remove the outer skin from the garlic bulbs and place the unpeeled cloves on a square of foil. Drizzle with 1 teaspoon olive oil. Bake at 350 degrees for 45 to 60 minutes. Cool to room temperature. Squeeze to remove the pulp from the skins.

Peel the potatoes and cut into halves. Soak in cold water for 5 minutes. Cook in salted water to cover in a saucepan for 15 minutes or until tender; drain. Combine with the garlic, butter and 2 tablespoons olive oil in a bowl. Add the half-and-half gradually, mixing until smooth and creamy.

Serves Four
Preparation Time: 15 minutes
Cooking Time: $1^{1}/4$ hours

Rosemary Potatoes with Garlic

The pungent flavor of garlic is the perfect foil for the bland flavor of potatoes. The rosemary, Worcestershire sauce and Dijon mustard in this dish also make it a lively addition to any meal.

Ingredients

1¹/2 pounds unpeeled small red potatoes
4 large unpeeled cloves of garlic
1 tablespoon olive oil
¹/2 teaspoon salt
4 sprigs fresh rosemary or 1 tablespoon dried rosemary
1 tablespoon white wine Worcestershire sauce
2 tablespoons Dijon mustard
3 tablespoons olive oil
¹/4 teaspoon pepper
2 or 3 green onions, thinly sliced

Directions

Scrub the unpeeled potatoes and cut into 1¹/2-inch pieces. Combine with the unpeeled garlic cloves, 1 tablespoon olive oil and salt in a medium bowl and toss to coat well. Place in a baking dish large enough to contain the potatoes in a single layer. Add the rosemary. Bake at 450 degrees for 30 to 40 minutes or until potatoes are tender and brown.

Whisk the Worcestershire sauce, mustard, 3 tablespoons olive oil and pepper in a bowl. Remove the rosemary sprigs and garlic from the baking dish, discarding the rosemary. Squeeze the garlic into the mustard mixture and mix well. Add to the potatoes with the green onions and mix lightly. Serve warm.

Serves Four
Preparation Time: 10 minutes
Cooking Time: 30 to 40 minutes

Sautéed Potatoes and Leeks

The Welsh have long appreciated the combination of potatoes and leeks. The Scots added a chicken to their favorite potato and leek concoction and called the resulting soup Cockaleekie. You will enjoy this simple combination of the two.

Ingredients

2 leek bulbs, sliced   2 tablespoons butter
4 or 5 large unpeeled baking potatoes, cooked
1/4 teaspoon celery seeds   Salt and pepper to taste
2 tablespoons chopped fresh parsley

Directions

Cook the leeks in the heated butter in a covered skillet over low heat for 8 to 10 minutes or until tender. Peel the potatoes and cut into thick slices. Add to the skillet and sprinkle with the celery seeds, salt and pepper. Cook, uncovered, for 7 to 8 minutes. Sprinkle with the parsley. Serve immediately.

Serves Four
Preparation Time: 10 minutes
Cooking Time: 15 to 20 minutes

Snow Peas and Carrots

Snow peas are delicious eaten fresh or cooked. In this dish, both the snow peas and the carrots are cooked just until they are tender-crisp, retaining some of the texture that adds to our enjoyment of them.

Ingredients

1 pound snow peas
3 large carrots, julienned
4 shallots, minced   2 tablespoons butter or margarine
2 tablespoons dry sherry
Salt and pepper to taste

Directions

Simmer the snow peas and carrots in water in a saucepan for 2 minutes. Rinse with cold water and drain. Sauté the shallots in the butter in a saucepan over medium heat for 1 minute. Add the snow peas and carrots. Cook for 1 minute longer. Sprinkle with the wine and cook for 3 minutes longer. Season with salt and pepper.

Serves Six
Preparation Time: 10 minutes
Cooking Time: 10 minutes

Spaghetti Squash Casserole

You can reduce the calories in any pasta recipe by substituting the long spaghetti-like strands of the spaghetti squash for the pasta.

Ingredients

1 spaghetti squash
1 cup small curd cottage cheese
1/2 cup shredded mozzarella cheese
1/2 cup grated fresh Parmesan cheese
2 medium onions, chopped
4 or 5 tomatoes, chopped
1 to 2 tablespoons dried basil
1 to 2 tablespoons dried oregano
Salt and pepper to taste

Directions

Pierce the squash with a fork. Cook in water to cover in a large saucepan for 40 minutes or until squash forks tender; drain. Cut into halves and cool to room temperature. Remove the strands of the squash to a bowl with a fork. Add the cheeses and mix well.

Sauté the onions and tomatoes with the basil, oregano, salt and pepper in a nonstick skillet until tender; drain if necessary. Add to the squash mixture and mix well. Spoon into a buttered baking dish. Bake at 350 degrees for 40 minutes or until bubbly.

Serves Twelve
Preparation Time: 15 minutes
Cooking Time: 1 hour and 20 minutes

Sweet Potato Chips

What could be more Southern than the combination of sweet potatoes and peanuts? These chips are easily prepared in the oven and are a delicious change from French-fried potatoes. Serve them with barbecued ribs and fried chicken, or as a great hors d'oeuvre.

Ingredients

3/4 cup honey-roasted peanuts
2 large sweet potatoes
1/2 cup melted butter
Salt to taste

Directions

Line a baking sheet with foil and spray with nonstick cooking spray. Process the peanuts in a food processor until finely chopped but not ground. Peel the sweet potatoes and cut into 1/8-inch slices. Dip in the butter, coating well on both sides. Arrange in a single layer on the prepared baking sheet. Sprinkle with the peanuts.

Bake at 475 degrees for 15 to 20 minutes or until the tops are light and the sweet potatoes are tender. Remove to paper towels for 5 minutes to drain and cool. Sprinkle with salt.

Serves Four
Preparation Time: 15 minutes
Cooking Time: 15 to 20 minutes

Orange-Baked Sweet Potatoes

For a special presentation, scoop the pulp from orange halves to make orange shells and spoon the baked sweet potatoes into the shells. Top with the marshmallows and bake just until light brown.

Ingredients

2 pounds unpeeled sweet potatoes or 1 (30-ounce) can, drained
Salt to taste
1/3 cup orange juice
1/2 teaspoon grated orange rind
1/4 cup packed brown sugar
2 tablespoons butter
1/4 teaspoon salt
1/4 cup chopped pecans or walnuts (optional)
1 cup miniature marshmallows

Directions

Cook the sweet potatoes in salted boiling water in a saucepan until tender. Peel and mash the potatoes in a bowl. Add the orange juice, orange rind, brown sugar, butter and 1/4 teaspoon salt. Beat until smooth, adding a small amount of milk if needed for desired consistency. Stir in the pecans.

Spoon into a greased shallow baking dish. Top with the marshmallows. Bake at 350 degrees just until golden brown.

Serves Eight
Preparation Time: 10 minutes
Cooking Time: 45 minutes

Caribbean Vegetable Medley

Garnish this dish with an island flower and enjoy the
tender-crisp crunch of a fresh medley.

Ingredients

4 ounces fresh green beans
1 cup sliced carrot
$1/4$ cup low-sodium chicken broth
2 tablespoon Chablis or Chardonnay
$1/4$ teaspoon curry powder
$1/8$ teaspoon white pepper
$1/2$ small red bell pepper, julienned
$1/3$ cup chopped onion
$11/2$ tablespoons unsweetened shredded coconut, toasted

Directions

Trim the beans and cut into 1-inch pieces. Combine with the carrot, chicken broth, wine, curry powder and white pepper in a 2-quart glass dish; cover with heavy-duty plastic wrap. Microwave on High for 6 minutes.

Add the bell pepper and onion. Microwave, covered, on High for 4 to 5 minutes or until the vegetables are tender-crisp. Sprinkle with the coconut.

Serves Four
Preparation Time: 10 minutes
Cooking Time: 10 minutes

Grilled Vegetables

The purpose of grilling is to impart flavor rather than to produce a quick meal, so remember not to place the grill too close to the fire or to set the gas on gas grills too high. Watch grilled foods carefully and allow time for even cooking.

Ingredients

3 Japanese eggplant
3 small to medium zucchini
3 red bell peppers
1 large red onion
1/4 cup olive oil
1 teaspoon oregano
Salt and pepper to taste
1 cup shredded mozzarella cheese

Directions

Slice the eggplant, zucchini and bell peppers into halves lengthwise; slice the onion 1/4 inch thick. Grill the vegetables over medium coals until tender-crisp, basting occasionally with half the olive oil.

Cut the vegetables into strips. Toss with the remaining olive oil, oregano, salt and pepper in a bowl, coating well. Add the cheese and toss again or sprinkle servings with the cheese.

Serves Eight
Preparation Time: 10 minutes
Cooking Time: 15 minutes

Vegetable Enchiladas

These are actually satisfying enough to serve as a main dish, but they also make an easy-to-prepare side dish to serve with the entrée.

Ingredients

1 Italian eggplant
1/2 medium onion, sliced
1/2 medium green bell pepper, sliced
1 tablespoon olive oil
2 medium zucchini, sliced
2 medium yellow squash, sliced
1 (8-ounce) can tomato sauce
1/2 cup picante sauce
8 flour tortillas
1 cup shredded Cheddar cheese

Directions

Peel and slice the eggplant and cut the slices into quarters. Sauté the onion and green pepper in the heated olive oil in a skillet for 5 minutes. Add the eggplant, zucchini and yellow squash. Sauté for 5 to 8 minutes longer or until tender-crisp. Stir in the tomato sauce and half the picante sauce. Simmer until the vegetables are tender.

Spoon enough of the mixture into a shallow baking dish to coat the bottom. Sprinkle half the cheese onto the tortillas and spoon the vegetable mixture over the cheese. Roll the tortillas to enclose the filling. Arrange in the prepared baking dish. Top with the remaining picante sauce and cheese. Bake at 350 degrees for 10 to 15 minutes or until heated through.

Serves Four
Preparation Time: 15 minutes
Cooking Time: 30 minutes

Fettuccini e Limone

The secret to pasta that stays hot while serving is to heat the oven-proof serving dish in a 200-degree oven for 10 minutes.

Ingredients

1 cup whipping cream
$1/4$ cup butter
2 tablespoons fresh lemon juice
Grated rind of 4 lemons
1 pound uncooked fresh fettuccini, fresh-dried or imported
Salt to taste
$1/2$ cup grated Parmesan cheese

Directions

Combine the cream and butter in a large skillet. Bring to a boil over high heat. Stir in the lemon juice and lemon rind. Cook until reduced by $1/2$, stirring constantly. Remove from heat.

Cook the pasta in salted boiling water in a saucepan and drain. Add to the skillet, tossing to coat well. Cook for 10 to 15 seconds. Combine with the cheese in the heated dish and toss lightly. Serve with additional cheese.

Serves Six
Preparation Time: 10 minutes
Cooking Time: 15 minutes

Vermicelli with Mascarpone and Spinach

Mascarpone is a buttery-rich creamy cheese from Italy's Lombardy region. It is a versatile cheese that blends well with other flavors, as it does here with the fresh spinach.

Ingredients

2 cloves of garlic
$1^1/_2$ tablespoons butter
10 ounces fresh spinach, finely chopped
5 ounces mascarpone cheese
$2/_3$ cup heavy cream
$1/_4$ cup (about) chicken stock
Lemon pepper to taste
16 ounces vermicelli, cooked *al dente*

Directions

Sauté the garlic in the butter in a skillet until golden brown. Add the spinach. Cook over low heat until tender, stirring frequently; discard the garlic.

Combine the mascarpone cheese with the cream and enough chicken stock to make of the desired consistency in a saucepan. Season with lemon pepper. Simmer for 3 minutes; drain. Combine with the pasta and spinach in a warm bowl and toss to coat well. Serve immediately.

Serves Six
Preparation Time: 10 minutes
Cooking Time: 15 minutes

Cilantro Pesto

*You will love this pesto with a south-of-the-border twist, using
cilantro, jalapeño pepper and pumpkin seeds.*

Ingredients

2 cups loosely packed fresh cilantro leaves
1 cup loosely packed parsley leaves
3/4 cup roasted salted pumpkin seeds
1/2 cup grated Parmesan cheese
1/2 cup lime juice   1 large jalapeño pepper
1 clove of garlic   3/4 cup vegetable oil

Directions

Combine the cilantro, parsley, pumpkin seeds, cheese, lime juice,
jalapeño pepper and garlic in a food processor. Process until smooth, scraping
sides occasionally. Add the oil gradually, processing constantly until smooth.

Cover the surface directly with plastic wrap and chill for up to 3 days.
Serve at room temperature over your favorite pasta.

Serves Six
Preparation Time: 10 minutes

Pasta with Pecan-Tomato Sauce

*This is a delicate sauce that is full of crunch and the summer flavor of fresh
tomatoes. Serve it with a bacon and spinach salad for a hot weather treat.*

Ingredients

4 large cloves of garlic, chopped
2/3 cup chopped pecans   1/2 cup butter
1 tablespoon best quality olive oil
3 medium fresh tomatoes, cut into 1-inch pieces
Salt and freshly ground pepper to taste
12 ounces fresh linguini, cooked

Directions

Sauté the garlic and pecans lightly in the melted butter and olive oil in
a large noncorrosive skillet for 2 minutes; do not brown. Add the tomatoes,
salt and pepper. Cook for 1 minute or until slightly thickened. Toss with the
hot pasta in a serving bowl. Serve with freshly grated Parmesan cheese.

Serves Four
Preparation Time: 5 minutes
Cooking Time: 5 minutes

Tortellini Pesto

Pesto is ready in minutes to serve over your favorite pasta. This version differs from the traditional pesto by the use of almonds in place of pine nuts.

Ingredients

36 basil leaves
4 cloves of garlic
5 ounces blanched almonds
1 1/4 cups grated Romano and Parmesan cheese in equal parts
7 ounces olive oil
Lemon pepper to taste
1 pound fresh tortellini, cooked

Directions

Combine the basil and garlic in the food processor and process until smooth. Add the almonds, cheese, olive oil and lemon pepper gradually, processing constantly.

Cook the pasta *al dente* using the package directions. Drain, reserving 3 tablespoons cooking liquid. Place in a serving bowl. Stir the reserved liquid into the pesto. Spoon over the pasta.

Serves Four
Preparation Time: 10 minutes
Cooking Time: 15 minutes

Sun-Dried Tomato Sauce for Pasta

Serve this sauce with freshly grated Parmesan cheese over a hearty pasta such as thick spaghetti or ziti. For an even heartier dish, add slices of lightly sautéed pepperoni to the sauce just before serving.

Ingredients

1/4 cup oil from jar of sun-dried tomatoes
1/4 cup unsalted butter
1 large yellow onion, chopped
3 stalks celery, chopped
3 carrots, peeled, chopped
3 cloves of garlic, minced
1 teaspoon fennel seeds
2 (28-ounce) cans tomatoes
3/4 cup chopped oil-pack sun-dried tomatoes
1 cup dry white wine
Salt and freshly ground pepper to taste

Directions

Heat the oil from the tomatoes and the butter in a skillet. Add the onion, celery, carrots, garlic and fennel seeds and sauté for 15 minutes. Stir in the undrained canned tomatoes, sun-dried tomatoes, wine, salt and pepper. Simmer for 1 hour, stirring occasionally.

Spoon into the food processor container and pulse just until finely chopped. Serve over pasta.

Serves Eight
Preparation Time: 15 minutes
Cooking Time: 1 1/4 hours

Brown and Wild Rice with Almonds and Ginger

This side dish also doubles as a salad and can be chilled until needed. The brown rice gives it a dense nutty flavor and provides valuable bran needed in our diet.

Ingredients

1 1/2 cups quick-cooking brown rice
1 cup quick-cooking wild rice
1 (10-ounce) package frozen green peas, thawed
1/2 cup thinly sliced scallions
1/4 cup chopped red bell pepper
1/4 to 1/3 cup canola oil
1/3 cup tarragon vinegar
3 tablespoons Dijon mustard
1 1/2 tablespoons freshly grated gingerroot
Salt to taste
1 teaspoon freshly ground pepper
2/3 cup sliced almonds, toasted

Directions

Cook the rice in 2 saucepans using the directions on the packages. Combine in a large bowl and cool. Add the peas, scallions and bell pepper.

Combine the oil, vinegar, mustard, ginger, salt and pepper in a small bowl and whisk until smooth. Add to the rice mixture and mix well. Add the almonds and toss lightly. Serve in a lettuce-lined bowl or individual serving plates.

Serves Ten
Preparation Time: 15 minutes
Cooking Time: 15 minutes

Fruited Rice Pilaf

Because rice is so rich in complex carbohydrates, low in fat and packed with vitamins, minerals, amino acids and fiber, it is predicted that our consumption will soon equal that of pasta. It can be deliciously combined with other flavors, as it is here, to offer infinite variety.

Ingredients

1 cup uncooked brown rice
2 cups vegetable stock or water
1/2 teaspoon salt
1/4 cup cashews
2 tablespoons butter or margarine
1/4 cup raisins
1/4 cup coarsely chopped dried apricots and dates

Directions

Bring the rice, vegetable stock and salt to a boil in a 2-quart saucepan and reduce the heat to low. Simmer for 45 minutes or until tender.

Toast the cashews in the butter in a small skillet over medium heat; remove with a slotted spoon. Add the raisins, apricots and dates to the skillet. Cook for 2 minutes. Stir into the rice. Let stand, covered, for 5 minutes. Stir in the cashews just before serving.

Serves Six
Preparation Time: 10 minutes
Cooking Time: 45 minutes

Harvest Rice

Add apples and raisins to rice for a delicious accompaniment to hearty pork and poultry dishes during the holidays.

Ingredients

1 cup thinly sliced carrots
1 tablespoon corn oil margarine
1 1/2 cups water
3/4 cup apple juice
2 tablespoons lemon juice
2 tablespoons light brown sugar
Salt to taste
1 cup uncooked rice
1/2 cup raisins
1/2 teaspoon cinnamon
2 cups sliced unpeeled apples
1/2 cup sliced green onions
1 tablespoon sesame seeds, toasted

Directions

Sauté the carrots in the margarine in a large skillet over low heat for 5 minutes or until tender-crisp. Add the water, apple juice, lemon juice, brown sugar and salt and mix well. Bring to a boil over medium heat.

Stir in the rice, raisins and cinnamon; cover and reduce the heat. Simmer for 15 minutes or until the rice is tender. Stir in the apples and green onions. Cook until heated through. Spoon into a serving dish and sprinkle with the sesame seeds.

Serves Six
Preparation Time: 10 minutes
Cooking Time: 20 minutes

Nutty Wild Rice

This dish needs to stand for two hours at room temperature before serving, so you can prepare it in advance and it will be ready to serve when you are, with no last-minute rush. To defat the canned chicken broth, chill it for several hours and remove the fat that congeals on the top.

Ingredients

1 cup uncooked wild rice
5$^1/_2$ cups defatted chicken broth
1 cup chopped pecans
1 cup golden raisins
Grated rind of 1 large orange
$^1/_3$ cup fresh orange juice
$^1/_4$ cup chopped fresh mint
4 scallions, thinly sliced
$^1/_4$ cup olive oil
1$^1/_2$ teaspoons salt
Freshly ground pepper to taste

Directions

Rinse the wild rice with cold water and combine with the chicken broth in a medium saucepan. Bring to a boil and reduce the heat. Simmer, uncovered, for 30 to 45 minutes or just until tender; drain.

Combine with the pecans, raisins, orange rind, orange juice, mint, scallions, olive oil, salt and pepper in a serving bowl and toss gently. Let stand for 2 hours to develop the flavors. Serve at room temperature.

Serves Eight
Preparation Time: 10 minutes, plus standing time
Cooking Time: 35 to 45 minutes

Baked Bananas

Southern climates the world over have long enjoyed fruit combined with or served with the main dish. Baked bananas are delicious served as a side dish, but they could also be served over ice cream.

Ingredients

6 bananas, sliced lengthwise
$1/2$ cup packed light brown sugar
$1/2$ cup unsalted butter
$1/2$ cup raisins
$1/2$ cup chopped pecans
1 tablespoon brandy

Directions

Arrange half the bananas in a buttered baking dish. Sprinkle with half the brown sugar, dot with half the butter, and sprinkle with half the raisins and pecans. Add the remaining brown sugar and butter. Top with the remaining bananas, raisins and pecans.

Bake at 350 degrees for 30 minutes. Pour the brandy over the layers and serve immediately.

Serves Six
Preparation Time: 10 minutes
Cooking Time: 30 minutes

Pineapple Bake

This is so easy to prepare in advance and bake just at dinner time to serve with ham or poultry. You can substitute two eggs and two egg whites for the four eggs to reduce the cholesterol.

Ingredients

1/2 cup butter, softened
1 cup sugar
4 eggs
1 (20-ounce) can crushed pineapple
4 or 5 slices bread, cubed

Directions

Cream the butter and sugar in a mixer bowl until light and fluffy. Add the eggs and beat for 3 to 4 minutes or until smooth.

Stir in the pineapple and bread. Spoon into a greased 2-quart baking dish. Bake at 350 degrees for 45 minutes.

Serves Four
Preparation Time: 10 minutes
Cooking Time: 45 minutes

Entrées

Beef

Beef on the Rocks, 135
Beef Rouladen*, 136
Grilled Beef Kabobs, 137
Grilled Flank Steak, 138
London Broil with Mushroom Sauce, 138

Pork

Bleu Cheese Pork Loin, 139
Herb–Marinated Pork Tenderloin, 139
Pork Loin with Apricots, 140
Pork Medallions in Mustard Sauce, 141
Pork Medallions with Sautéed Apples, 142
Grilled Garlic Pork Chops, 143
Grilled Marinated Sweet and Sour Pork, 144

Veal

Breaded Veal with Lemon and Capers, 145
Veal Chops Italiano, 146
Veal Scalopini, 147

Poultry

Brown Bag Chicken, 148
Parmesan Baked Chicken, 149
Chicken and Asparagus Pinwheels, 150
Cajun Chicken and Mushrooms, 151
Citrus Chicken Stir–Fry, 152
Gorgonzola Chicken, 153
Jamaican Chicken, 154
Spicy Kung Pao Chicken, 155
Lime and Cilantro Chicken with Tomato Salsa, 156
Normandy Chicken, 157
Orange–Glazed Chicken, 158
Chicken in Pastry Shells, 159
Spinach–Stuffed Chicken in Apricot Sauce, 160
Chicken with Sun–Dried Tomato Sauce, 161
Versatile Baked Chicken, 162
Turkey Enchiladas, 163
Rock Cornish Game Hens with Wild Rice, 164

*Photograph Recipe
Cilantro Pesto for pasta on page 124
Savory Bread on page 53
Wine: Simi, Cabernet Sauvignon, 1990

Beef on the Rocks

The thickness of this cut of beef makes it a good candidate for grilling; even inexperienced cooks are likely to get a succulent result with this recipe. Leftovers make wonderful steak salad on the second day.

Ingredients

2 tablespoons ground ginger
$^1/_2$ cup salt
$^1/_4$ cup ground pepper
1 (4-pound) eye of round roast
7 cloves of garlic

Directions

Mix the ginger, salt and pepper in a small bowl. Make 7 slits in the roast with a sharp knife and insert the cloves of garlic. Press the ginger mix over the entire surface. Let stand at room temperature for 3 hours. Grill over hot coals with lid closed for 15 minutes. Turn the roast and grill for 12 minutes. Turn the roast again and grill for 12 minutes longer for medium rare. Slice to serve.

Serves Eight
Preparation Time: 10 minutes, plus standing time
Cooking Time: 40 minutes

Beef Rouladen

*Rouladen is the German version of the dish which consists of
thin pieces of beef rolled around a filling. The French version is called
paupiettes and the Italian, bracioli.*

Ingredients

2 or 3 onions, sliced into rings
2 tablespoons water
4 slices bacon
4 slices round steak
2 tablespoons mustard
Salt and pepper to taste
2 pickles, sliced lengthwise into quarters
1 large onion, chopped
2 teaspoons crushed garlic
2 (10-ounce) cans consommé
1 carrot, chopped
1 stalk celery, chopped
2 cups sliced mushrooms
$1/2$ cup red wine

Directions

Steam the sliced onions in the water in a saucepan until tender. Sauté
the bacon in a heavy saucepan until partially cooked. Remove the bacon to
drain, reserving the drippings. Pound the steak $1/4$ inch thick with a meat
mallet. Spread 1 side with mustard and season with salt and pepper. Spoon
the onions onto the steak pieces and top with 1 slice of bacon and 2 pieces
of pickle. Roll each piece to enclose the filling and secure lengthwise and
crosswise with string. Brown the rolls in the drippings in the saucepan and
remove to a plate. Sauté the chopped onion and garlic in the drippings in the
saucepan. Add the consommé, carrot, celery and mushrooms. Add the beef
rolls and wine. Simmer for 1 hour. You may thicken the sauce with a mixture
of flour and water to serve with the rouladen.

Serves Four
Preparation Time: 20 minutes
Cooking Time: $1 1/2$ hours

Grilled Beef Kabobs

Kabobs lend themselves perfectly to picnics or patio parties.
Alternate the beef, or other meat, with the vegetables of your choice and
serve them directly from the skewer on a bed of rice, kasha,
bulgur, watercress or shredded lettuce.

For the marinade

$1/2$ cup vegetable oil
$3/4$ cup soy sauce
$1/2$ cup Worcestershire sauce
$1/3$ cup fresh lemon juice
2 cloves of garlic, minced
2 tablespoons dry mustard
$2^{1}/_2$ teaspoons salt
1 tablespoon coarsely ground pepper

For the kabobs

2 pounds boneless sirloin tip or rump roast, cut into 2-inch pieces
1 cup unpeeled small red potatoes, parboiled
1 cup large mushrooms
1 cup small onions
1 cup cherry tomatoes

To prepare the marinade

Combine the oil, soy sauce, Worcestershire sauce, lemon juice, garlic, dry mustard, salt and pepper in a blender or food processor; process until smooth.

To prepare the kabobs

Add the beef to the marinade and mix well. Marinate in the refrigerator for 8 hours; drain. Soak bamboo skewers in water. Alternate the beef with the potatoes, mushrooms, onions and tomatoes on the skewers. Grill for 15 minutes or until the beef is done to taste.

Serves Four
Preparation Time: 15 minutes, plus marinating time
Cooking Time: 15 minutes

Grilled Flank Steak

*Flank steak can be a surprisingly economical cut
of beef to serve because there is no waste.*

Ingredients

¹/₄ cup soy sauce   ¹/₄ cup white wine, sherry or sake
2 tablespoons sesame oil
3 tablespoons melted butter or margarine   2 tablespoons sugar
2 cloves of garlic, minced   1 tablespoon freshly grated ginger
¹/₂ cup barbecue sauce   1 (2-pound) flank steak

Directions

Process the first 7 ingredients in a food processor and process until
smooth. Combine with the barbecue sauce in a sealable plastic bag or shallow
dish. Add the steak, coating well. Marinate in the refrigerator for 4 hours or
longer. Drain, reserving the marinade. Grill the steak for 10 minutes on each
side. Boil the reserved marinade in a saucepan for 3 to 4 minutes or until
heated through. Slice the steak thinly across the grain. Serve with the marinade.

Serves Six
Preparation Time: 10 minutes, plus marinating time
Cooking Time: 20 minutes

London Broil with Mushroom Sauce

*Score the steak in a diamond pattern on both sides to better absorb the
marinade. Remember that a London broil steak can become tough if it is
cooked too long and is better served rare or medium-rare.*

Ingredients

¹/₂ cup olive oil   ¹/₂ cup soy sauce
¹/₄ cup balsamic vinegar   8 cloves of garlic
4 teaspoons dried rosemary   1 (2-to 3-pound) London broil steak
1 pound fresh mushrooms, sliced   1 teaspoon butter or margarine

Directions

Combine the olive oil, soy sauce, vinegar, garlic and rosemary in a blender
and process until smooth. Combine with the steak in a sealable plastic bag
and coat well. Marinate in the refrigerator for 6 to 8 hours. Drain, reserving
the marinade. Grill the steak until done to taste. Sauté the mushrooms in the
butter in a saucepan. Add the reserved marinade. Cook until heated through.
Slice the steak and serve with the warm sauce.

Serves Six
Preparation Time: 10 minutes, plus marinating time
Cooking Time: 20 minutes

Bleu Cheese Pork Loin

The pork industry has successfully reduced the ratio of meat to fat and today a three-ounce serving contains 24 grams of protein and only 6 grams of fat as compared to 16 grams of fat in 2 tablespoons of peanut butter.

Ingredients

1 (3- to 4-pound) pork loin
6 cloves of garlic, minced   8 ounces bleu cheese
Salt and pepper to taste

Directions

Bake the pork loin at 300 degrees in a large baking dish for 1 hour. Slice a pocket in the pork, cutting to but not through the bottom and leaving 1 inch at each end. Rub the garlic over the outside and cut sides of the pork. Spread the cheese evenly in the pocket. Season with salt and pepper. Increase the oven temperature to 325 degrees. Bake for 45 to 60 minutes longer or until cooked through.

Serves Ten
Preparation Time: 10 minutes
Cooking Time: 2 hours

Herb-Marinated Pork Tenderloin

Boneless cuts of pork like the tenderloin are a good value, because they provide four to six servings per pound—in addition to good flavor.

Ingredients

1/2 cup soy sauce   3 tablespoons brown sugar
5 cloves of garlic, sliced
2 tablespoons dried cilantro
1 teaspoon dry mustard   1 teaspoon ground cumin
1/2 teaspoon paprika
1 (12- to 16-ounce) pork tenderloin

Directions

Combine the soy sauce, brown sugar, garlic, cilantro, dry mustard, cumin and paprika in a large sealable plastic bag and mix well. Add the pork tenderloin to the bag. Marinate in the refrigerator for 1 to 24 hours; drain. Grill over medium-hot coals for 20 to 30 minutes or until cooked through.

Serves Four
Preparation Time: 30 minutes, plus marinating time
Cooking Time: 20 to 30 minutes

Pork Loin with Apricots

*The flavor of fruit enhances pork dishes and has
traditionally been served with pork. This recipe is just as delicious
with prunes, or with prunes and apricots.*

Ingredients

18 dried apricots
1 (5-pound) boned pork loin, rolled and tied
Salt and freshly ground white pepper to taste
2 cups hot water
3 tablespoons flour
1³/₄ cups chicken broth
3 tablespoons sherry (optional)

Directions

Soak the apricots in water to cover in a bowl for 30 minutes; drain. Cut a deep slit in the pork with a sharp knife and insert half the apricots. Secure the slit with string or a skewer. Season with salt and white pepper.

Place in a greased baking pan and add 2 cups hot water. Bake at 350 degrees for 3 hours or to 190 degrees on a meat thermometer.

Combine the remaining apricots with water to cover in a small saucepan. Bring to a boil and simmer for 20 minutes or until tender.

Remove the pork to a heated platter and keep warm. Measure 3 tablespoons of drippings from the pork into a saucepan. Blend in the flour. Cook until smooth and brown, stirring constantly. Stir in the chicken broth gradually. Cook until thickened, stirring constantly. Stir in the wine, salt and white pepper. Drain the apricots and arrange around the pork. Serve with the sauce.

Serves Fifteen
Preparation Time: 20 minutes, plus soaking time
Cooking Time: 3¹/₄ hours

Pork Medallions in Mustard Sauce

Coarse-grained German mustards, such as Dusseldorf, are second in popularity only to Dijon mustard and are especially compatible with pork dishes, which are also a German favorite.

For the pork

2 tablespoons oil
2 tablespoons coarse-grained mustard
$1/2$ teaspoon salt
$1/2$ teaspoon pepper
2 (12-ounce) pork tenderloins
$1/4$ cup dry white wine

For the mustard sauce

$13/4$ cups whipping cream
$1/4$ cup coarse-grained mustard
$1/4$ teaspoon salt
$1/8$ teaspoon white pepper

To prepare the pork

Combine the oil, mustard, salt and pepper in a bowl and mix well. Rub over the pork and place in a sealable plastic bag. Marinate in the refrigerator for 8 hours. Place the pork on a rack in a shallow roasting pan. Insert a meat thermometer into the thickest part. Roast at 375 degrees for 25 minutes or to 160 degrees on the meat thermometer, basting with the wine every 10 minutes. Cut into $3/4$-inch slices and arrange on dinner plates; keep warm.

To prepare the mustard sauce

Heat the whipping cream in a heavy saucepan for 15 minutes or until reduced to $11/4$ cups; do not boil. Stir in the mustard, salt and white pepper. Spoon around the pork to serve.

Serves Four
Preparation Time: 15 minutes, plus marinating time
Cooking Time: 30 minutes

Pork Medallions with Sautéed Apples

Serve this with a side-dish of sweet and sour red cabbage and a crusty bread for a hearty meal sure to please family and guests alike.

1 (16-ounce) pork tenderloin
2 eggs
1 tablespoon water
3/4 cup bread crumbs
3/4 cup grated Parmesan cheese
1/4 cup flour
5 tablespoons butter
2 large Golden Delicious apples, peeled, sliced
4 shallots, chopped
Salt and pepper to taste
1/4 cup chicken broth

Directions

Slice the pork diagonally 1/2 inch thick. Pound the slices 1/8 inch thick with a meat mallet. Beat the eggs with the water in a shallow dish. Mix the bread crumbs and cheese together. Coat the pork with the flour, shaking off the excess. Dip into the egg mixture and coat with the bread crumb mixture. Cook in several batches in 4 tablespoons butter in a large skillet for 3 minutes on each side or until light brown. Remove to a platter with a slotted spoon and keep warm.

Melt the remaining 1 tablespoon butter in the same skillet. Add the apples and shallots. Sauté for 5 minutes or until tender. Season with salt and pepper. Stir in the chicken broth. Simmer for 5 minutes or until thickened. Spoon around the pork.

Serves Six
Preparation Time: 10 minutes
Cooking Time: 15 minutes

Grilled Garlic Pork Chops

*Add black beans and rice and the sections of fresh oranges for
a menu with the flavor of the islands.*

Ingredients

1/2 cup garlic cloves
1 cup water
1/2 cup olive oil
1/4 cup cider vinegar
Juice of 1 large lemon
1/2 teaspoon dried thyme or cilantro
2 teaspoons salt
1/2 teaspoon cayenne pepper
8 thick (8-ounce) pork chops

Directions

Blanch the garlic in boiling water in a saucepan for 4 minutes. Drain
and chop the garlic. Combine with the olive oil, vinegar, lemon juice, thyme,
salt and cayenne pepper in a shallow dish and mix well.

Add the pork chops, turning to coat well. Marinate in the refrigerator
for 4 to 6 hours; drain. Grill the pork chops over medium-hot coals until
cooked through.

Serves Eight
Preparation Time: 15 minutes, plus marinating time
Cooking Time: 20 minutes

Grilled Marinated Sweet and Sour Pork

Enjoy the flavor of the classic pork favorite with the ease of grilling.

Ingredients

3/4 cup fresh lemon juice
1/2 cup soy sauce
6 tablespoons honey
2 small shallots, coarsely chopped
2 large cloves of garlic, cut into halves
2 bay leaves, crumbled
1 teaspoon dry mustard
1/2 teaspoon ground ginger
2 teaspoons salt
2 teaspoons pepper
4 (12-ounce) pork tenderloins

Directions

Combine the lemon juice, soy sauce, honey, shallots, garlic, bay leaves, dry mustard, ginger, salt and pepper in a blender and process until smooth. Place the pork tenderloins in 2 sealable plastic bags and add half the marinade to each bag. Marinate in the refrigerator for 8 hours, turning occasionally.

Drain the marinade into a saucepan. Grill the pork over medium-high heat for 20 minutes for medium, turning frequently.

Cook the reserved marinade for 5 minutes or until reduced to the desired consistency. Slice the pork and serve with the sauce.

Serves Twelve
Preparation Time: 10 minutes, plus marinating time
Cooking Time: 25 minutes

Breaded Veal with Lemon and Capers

Pinot Blanc or Chardonnay make a perfect accompaniment to this beautiful presentation.

Ingredients

4 (4-ounce) veal scalopini
2 eggs, lightly beaten
3 tablespoons water
Salt and freshly ground pepper to taste
1 cup flour
1 cup bread crumbs
$1/4$ to $1/2$ cup vegetable oil
6 tablespoons butter
1 hard-cooked egg, chopped
$1/4$ cup finely chopped parsley

Garnish

Capers
4 thin slices lemon

Directions

Pound the veal flat between 2 pieces of waxed paper. Beat the eggs with the water, salt and pepper in a shallow dish. Coat each piece of veal with flour, dip into the egg mixture and coat with the bread crumbs. Heat $1/4$ cup oil in a large skillet. Add the veal and cook for 3 minutes on each side or until golden brown, adding additional oil if needed. Remove the veal to a warmed platter; keep warm.

Add the butter to the drippings in the skillet. Cook until light brown, swirling to keep from burning. Drizzle over the veal. Sprinkle with the chopped egg and parsley. Garnish with capers and lemon slices.

Serves Four
Preparation Time: 10 minutes
Cooking Time: 10 minutes

Veal Chops Italiano

*The intensely cultivated landscape of the Italian countryside
allows very little opportunity for animal husbandry, so the Italians have
become expert in dishes that use the younger animals, or veal. You
will appreciate this example of the art.*

Ingredients

3/4 cup packed fresh basil leaves
1 tablespoon pinenuts, toasted
1 tablespoon grated Parmesan cheese
1 clove of garlic
1/4 cup nonfat plain yogurt
1/2 teaspoon oregano
4 (6-ounce) lean veal chops, 3/4 inch thick, trimmed
4 slices tomato
4 (1/2-ounce) slices fontina or provolone cheese

Garnish

1/4 cup chopped parsley

Directions

Process the basil, pinenuts, cheese and garlic in a food processor until
well chopped. Combine with the yogurt and oregano in a small bowl and mix
well. Chill, covered, for 30 minutes.

Place the veal chops on a broiler pan sprayed with nonstick cooking
spray. Broil 5 to 6 inches from the heat source for 5 minutes on each side.
Spread with the basil mixture. Broil for 5 minutes longer. Top each chop with
1 slice of tomato and 1 slice of cheese. Broil for 2 to 3 minutes longer or until
the cheese melts. Garnish with parsley.

Serves Four
Preparation Time: 10 minutes, plus chilling time
Cooking Time: 15 to 18 minutes

Veal Scalopini

Veal is best when cooked quickly, as it is here, or with a wine or tomato-based sauce, because it is so lean that it can easily become dry. The flavor of lemon has a natural affinity for the delicate flavor of the veal.

Ingredients

4 veal scalopini
$1/2$ cup buttermilk
$3/4$ cup yellow cornmeal
$1/2$ teaspoon freshly ground pepper
1 tablespoon margarine
2 tablespoons (or more) olive oil
1 teaspoon margarine
$1/4$ cup fresh lemon juice
4 thin lemon slices
2 tablespoons chopped parsley
$1/2$ cup chopped seeded tomato

Directions

Pound the veal very thin with a meat mallet. Dip in the buttermilk and coat lightly with a mixture of the cornmeal and pepper. Melt 1 tablespoon margarine with the olive oil in a nonstick skillet over low heat. Increase the heat to medium and add half the veal. Cook for 2 minutes on each side or until golden brown. Repeat with the remaining veal, adding additional oil if needed. Remove the veal to a warm serving platter and drain the skillet.

Melt 1 teaspoon margarine in the skillet and stir in the lemon juice, lemon slices and half the parsley. Cook over medium heat for 1 minute, swirling the skillet several times. Drizzle over the veal. Top with the tomato and remaining parsley.

Serves Four
Preparation Time: 10 minutes
Cooking Time: 10 minutes

Brown Bag Chicken

*Always use a bag made of nonrecycled material, as heating
can release toxic chemicals in recycled paper.*

Ingredients

1 (2- to 3-pound) chicken
1 teaspoon paprika
$1/2$ teaspoon onion powder
$1/4$ teaspoon garlic powder
$1/2$ teaspoon thyme
2 teaspoons salt
$1/4$ teaspoon black pepper
$3/4$ teaspoon cayenne pepper
$1/4$ teaspoon white pepper

Directions

Rinse the chicken inside and out and pat dry. Combine the paprika, onion powder, garlic powder, thyme, salt, black pepper, cayenne pepper and white pepper in a bowl and mix well. Rub on the chicken inside and out. Place in a plastic bag and chill in the refrigerator for 8 hours.

Remove the chicken from the plastic bag and tie the legs together. Place in a brown paper bag made of new material and twist the opening to close. Place on a low oven rack and place a baking sheet on a rack below the chicken. Roast at 400 degrees for $1 1/2$ hours without opening the bag.

Serves Four
Preparation Time: 10 minutes, plus chilling time
Cooking Time: $1 1/2$ hours

Parmesan Baked Chicken

This is such an easy dish to prepare for the family on busy nights, but it is also a good dish for guests, as it requires so little time and effort at serving time.

Ingredients

3 pounds chicken, cut up
1 tablespoon vegetable oil
Salt and pepper to taste
$^1/_4$ cup grated Parmesan cheese

Directions

Rinse the chicken and pat dry. Spread the oil in a roasting pan and arrange the chicken skin side down in the pan; season with salt and pepper.

Roast at 400 degrees for 15 minutes. Turn the chicken and sprinkle with the cheese. Roast for 20 to 25 minutes longer or until the chicken is golden brown and cooked through.

Serves Four
Preparation Time: 10 minutes
Cooking Time: 35 to 40 minutes

Chicken and Asparagus Pinwheels

This dish makes a beautiful presentation and the leftovers are just as delicious cold, alone or atop a spring salad.

For the marinade

1/4 cup dry white wine
1 tablespoon fresh lemon juice
1 tablespoon minced fresh sage
1/8 teaspoon ground white pepper

For the chicken

4 boneless skinless chicken breast halves
8 thin (4-inch) asparagus stalks, lightly blanched
1/2 cup flour
1 tablespoon safflower oil
1 cup coarsely chopped asparagus, lightly blanched
1/2 cup chicken broth, heated
1 teaspoon cornstarch
1 teaspoon water
1 tablespoon unsalted butter
Ground red pepper to taste

To prepare the marinade

Combine the wine, lemon juice, sage and white pepper in a medium glass bowl and mix well.

To prepare the chicken

Rinse the chicken and pat dry. Arrange 2 asparagus stalks at 1 end of each piece of chicken and roll to enclose; secure with wooden picks. Add to the marinade, coating well. Chill for 2 hours. Drain, reserving the marinade. Pat the chicken dry and coat lightly with the flour. Brown lightly in the heated oil in an ovenproof skillet over medium heat. Add the marinade. Bake, covered, at 350 degrees for 10 minutes or until the juices run clear when the chicken is pierced in the thickest part; remove to a platter.

Purée the chopped asparagus with the hot chicken broth in a blender. Strain into a small saucepan. Stir in a mixture of the cornstarch and water. Cook until thickened, stirring constantly. Whisk in the butter and red pepper. Remove the wooden picks from the chicken and cut into 1/3-inch slices. Spoon 2 tablespoons of the asparagus sauce onto each of 4 serving plates. Arrange the chicken and asparagus pinwheels in an overlapping layer in the sauce.

Serves Four
Preparation Time: 20 minutes, plus chilling time
Cooking Time: 20 minutes

Cajun Chicken and Mushrooms

*The seasoning in this dish gives it a hint of the spicy cooking
of Louisiana, but you can vary the seasoning to suit your tastes.*

Ingredients

$1/2$ cup flour
$1/2$ teaspoon paprika
$1/2$ teaspoon basil
$1/2$ teaspoon garlic powder
$1/4$ teaspoon dry mustard
$1/4$ teaspoon black pepper
$1/2$ teaspoon cayenne pepper
4 boneless chicken breasts
2 tablespoons melted butter
2 green onions, chopped
8 ounces mushrooms, cut into halves
$1^{1}/2$ cups chicken stock, heated
1 tablespoon cornstarch
3 tablespoons cold water
$1/2$ cup sour cream

Directions

Mix the flour, paprika, basil, garlic powder, dry mustard, black pepper
and cayenne pepper in a shallow dish. Rinse the chicken well and coat with
the flour mixture. Brown in the melted butter in a skillet over medium heat
for 5 minutes. Add the green onions and mushrooms. Cook for 2 minutes.
Add the chicken stock. Cook for 2 minutes.

Remove the chicken to a warm platter. Cook the mixture in the skillet
for 8 minutes longer. Stir in a mixture of the cornstarch and water. Cook over
high heat for 1 minute or until thickened, stirring constantly. Remove from
heat. Stir in the sour cream. Add the chicken.

Serves Four
Preparation Time: 5 minutes
Cooking Time: 25 minutes

Citrus Chicken Stir-Fry

The fresh, crisp taste of the citrus juices gives this dish a unique flavor.
Serve it over rice and add a garnish of frosted grapes.

Ingredients

8 ounces boneless skinless chicken breasts
2 tablespoons flour
Salt and freshly ground pepper to taste
2 carrots, peeled, julienned
2 tablespoons corn oil margarine
Juice of 1 orange
Juice of $1/2$ lemon
1 teaspoon crumbled dried rosemary
2 tablespoons chopped fresh parsley

Directions

Cut the chicken into bite-sized pieces; rinse and pat dry. Coat with a mixture of flour, salt and pepper. Stir-fry the chicken and the carrots in the melted margarine in a skillet over medium-high heat for 3 to 5 minutes or until cooked through.

Add the orange juice, lemon juice and rosemary. Cook for 2 minutes longer, stirring constantly. Sprinkle with parsley. Serve over rice.

Serves Two
Preparation Time: 10 minutes
Cooking Time: 8 minutes

Gorgonzola Chicken

*Gorgonzola cheese, named for the town outside Milan where it originated,
is a semisoft cow's or goat's cheese. It is ivory in color with bluish-green
veins and a pungent bleu cheese flavor and aroma.*

Ingredients

6 (5-ounce) boneless, skinless chicken breast halves
$1/2$ cup flour
1 teaspoon salt
$1/2$ teaspoon pepper
1 medium onion, chopped
$1/4$ cup chopped fresh parsley
$1/3$ cup extra-virgin olive oil
Juice of $1/2$ lemon
1 cup chicken stock
$1/2$ cup white Rhine wine
10 to 12 ounces gorgonzola cheese

Directions

Rinse the chicken and pat dry. Pound very thin with a meat mallet. Coat lightly with a mixture of the flour, salt and pepper. Sauté the onion and parsley in the heated olive oil in a large skillet until tender; remove with a slotted spoon.

Add the chicken and sauté for 3 minutes on each side or until golden brown. Add the onion mixture, lemon juice, chicken stock, wine and cheese. Simmer, covered, for 10 to 15 minutes. Cook, uncovered, until the sauce is reduced by $1/2$, turning chicken occasionally.

Serves Six
Preparation Time: 10 minutes
Cooking Time: 30 minutes

Jamaican Chicken

Chicken is one of the world's most popular forms of protein and one of the most popular in Jamaica, which gives a tropical twist to this versatile favorite.

For the marinade

$1/4$ cup lime juice
$1/4$ cup lemon juice
$1/2$ cup white wine
$1/4$ cup sweet vermouth
$1/4$ cup Worcestershire sauce
2 tablespoons Dijon mustard
$1/4$ teaspoon ground cumin
$1/4$ teaspoon dried basil
$1/4$ teaspoon dried oregano
1 teaspoon Old Bay seasoning
$1/4$ teaspoon freshly ground pepper

For the chicken

4 whole chicken breasts, skinned
2 tablespoons Dijon mustard
$1 1/2$ tablespoons butter

To prepare the marinade

Combine the lime juice, lemon juice, white wine, vermouth, Worcestershire sauce, mustard, cumin, basil, oregano, Old Bay seasoning and pepper in a bowl; mix well.

To prepare the chicken

Rinse the chicken and pat dry. Arrange in a 9x13-inch baking dish. Pour the marinade over the chicken. Marinate, covered, in the refrigerator for 1 hour or longer. Drain and reserve the marinade. Rub the chicken with the mustard and butter and return to the baking dish. Add the marinade. Bake at 350 degrees for 45 minutes, basting occasionally. Remove the chicken to a serving platter. Serve with the pan juices and French bread for dipping.

Serves Four
Preparation Time: 10 minutes, plus marinating time
Cooking Time: 45 minutes

Spicy Kung Pao Chicken

*Look for the bean sauce, hoisin sauce and chili paste with garlic
in an Asian market or a well-stocked supermarket. They will give an
authentic flavor to the spicy Chinese dish.*

Ingredients

1 pound skinless boneless chicken breasts
1 egg white, lightly beaten
2 teaspoons cornstarch
2 tablespoons bean sauce
1 tablespoon hoisin sauce
1 tablespoon chili paste with garlic
1 tablespoon sherry
1 tablespoon red wine vinegar
1 teaspoon sugar
3 cloves of garlic, chopped
1/4 cup peanut oil
2 or 3 dried chili peppers (optional)
1/2 cup chopped celery
1 cup chopped zucchini
1 cup unsalted peanuts
4 cups cooked rice

Directions

Cut the chicken into 3/4-inch pieces; rinse and pat dry. Combine with
the egg white and cornstarch in a bowl and mix well. Chill in the refrigerator
for 30 minutes. Combine the bean sauce, hoisin sauce, chili paste, wine,
vinegar, sugar and garlic in a bowl and mix well; set aside. Stir-fry the chicken
in half the heated peanut oil in a wok or heavy skillet over high heat for 2 to
3 minutes or until cooked through; do not overcook or brown. Remove the
chicken and wipe the wok.

Heat the remaining peanut oil in the wok and add the chili peppers.
Stir-fry for 1 minute or until dark brown. Add the celery and zucchini. Stir-fry
for 2 minutes. Add the chicken and sauce mixture. Cook for 2 to 3 minutes.
Add the peanuts and toss lightly. Discard the chili peppers. Serve over
the rice.

Serves Four
Preparation Time: 15 minutes, plus chilling time
Cooking Time: 10 to 12 minutes

Lime and Cilantro Chicken with Tomato Salsa

Salsa is one of the fastest-growing products in the United States, passing catsup in dollar sales. This easy version has a wonderful fresh taste and could be used in other dishes or as a "skinny dip."

For the salsa

3 jalapeño peppers, seeded, cut into quarters
2 large tomatoes, cut into quarters
2 green onions, sliced
1 teaspoon wine or cider vinegar

For the chicken

4 skinless boneless chicken breasts
3 cloves of garlic, minced
2 green onions, thinly sliced
1 tablespoon fresh lime juice
2 tablespoons chopped cilantro
Freshly ground pepper to taste
1 avocado, peeled, sliced

Garnish

Chopped fresh cilantro

To prepare the salsa

Combine the peppers, tomatoes, green onions and vinegar in a blender or food processor and process until smooth. Chill for 1 hour or longer.

To prepare the chicken

Cut the chicken breasts into halves, rinse and pat dry. Arrange in a baking dish and sprinkle with garlic, green onions, lime juice, cilantro and pepper. Bake at 350 degrees for 30 to 40 minutes or until cooked through. Remove to 4 serving plates and arrange avocado slices next to chicken. Spoon salsa onto plates. Garnish with fresh cilantro.

Serves Four
Preparation Time: 10 minutes, plus chilling time
Cooking Time: 30 to 40 minutes

Normandy Chicken

*Normandy is famous for apples and for apple brandy, called
Calvados, which is often teamed with chicken in regional cooking. For an
authentic touch, use Calvados for the optional brandy in this dish
and serve it with honey-poached apples.*

Ingredients

6 boneless skinless chicken breast halves
3 tablespoons butter or margarine
2 tablespoons olive oil
1 (12- to 16-ounce) jar whole boiled onions
1 (10-ounce) can chicken broth
$1/2$ cup apple juice
$1/2$ teaspoon thyme
$1/2$ teaspoon salt
$1/2$ teaspoon pepper
$1/2$ cup half-and-half
3 tablespoons cornstarch
2 tablespoons brandy (optional)

Directions

Rinse the chicken and pat dry. Pound $1/2$ inch thick between sheets of
waxed paper. Brown on both sides in the heated butter and olive oil in a large
skillet over high heat. Add the onions, chicken broth, apple juice, thyme, salt
and pepper. Reduce the heat to medium. Simmer, covered, for 10 minutes or
until tender, turning once. Remove the chicken and onions to a warm platter.

Bring the pan juices to a boil, scraping the skillet to deglaze. Cook for
5 minutes or until reduced to $1/2$ cup. Reduce the heat to medium. Whisk the
half-and-half, cornstarch and brandy in a small bowl. Add to the skillet
gradually. Cook for 2 minutes or until thickened, stirring constantly. Spoon
over the chicken.

Serves Six
Preparation Time: 10 minutes
Cooking Time: 30 minutes

Orange-Glazed Chicken

*The sun-drenched taste of Florida oranges adds a delightful flavor
to almost any dish. This one is quick and easy enough for a family dinner
and good enough for company.*

Ingredients

4 boneless skinless chicken breasts
$1/2$ cup flour
Salt and pepper to taste
$1/4$ cup butter or margarine
$1/4$ cup orange juice

Directions

Rinse the chicken and pat dry. Coat with a mixture of the flour, salt and pepper. Brown in the butter in a skillet over medium heat. Remove to a warm platter.

Stir the orange juice into the pan drippings. Cook until thickened to desired consistency. Spoon over the chicken.

Serves Four
Preparation Time: 5 minutes
Cooking Time: 15 minutes

Chicken in Pastry Shells

*This is not your grandmother's creamed chicken! The sauce
has a generous addition of Dijon mustard and the frozen puff pastry
shells eliminate much of the work.*

Ingredients

2 whole boneless skinless chicken breasts
2 cups chicken broth
8 frozen puff pastry shells
1/3 cup Dijon mustard
3 tablespoons red wine vinegar
1/4 cup vegetable oil
1 1/2 tablespoons crumbled dried tarragon
1 teaspoon ground celery seed
1/2 teaspoon salt
Freshly ground pepper to taste
1/2 cup plus 2 tablespoons light cream
1 (8-ounce) can sliced water chestnuts, drained
1 cup thinly sliced green onions
1/3 cup finely chopped pimento
1 cup shredded Gruyère or Swiss cheese

Directions

Cut the chicken breasts into halves and rinse well. Combine with the
chicken broth and enough water to cover in a large saucepan. Simmer for 10
minutes or until the chicken is tender. Drain the chicken, cool slightly and
cut into 3/4-inch pieces.

Cook the pastry shells using the package directions. Combine the
mustard and vinegar in a bowl and mix well. Add the oil gradually, beating
constantly until the mixture is thick and smooth. Season with the tarragon,
celery seed, salt and pepper. Whisk in the cream. Stir in the water chestnuts,
green onions, pimento and chicken.

Spoon into the pastry shells on a baking sheet; sprinkle with the cheese.
Bake at 350 degrees for 12 to 15 minutes or until heated through and cheese
melts. Serve immediately.

Serves Eight
Preparation Time: 10 minutes
Cooking Time: 25 to 30 minutes

Spinach-Stuffed Chicken in Apricot Sauce

*In addition to the method given here, this can also be prepared
by stuffing the spinach mixture into pockets cut in chicken breasts.
The fresh apricots in season are delicious in this dish,
but plumped dried apricots can be used as well.*

Ingredients

1 (10-ounce) package frozen chopped spinach, thawed
$^1/_2$ cup 1% fat cottage cheese
$^1/_3$ cup bread crumbs
1 tablespoon minced shallot
1 egg white
$^1/_8$ teaspoon garlic powder
$^1/_8$ teaspoon nutmeg
Salt to taste
6 (4-ounce) boneless skinless chicken breast halves
1 tablespoon vegetable oil
1 cup apricot nectar
3 tablespoons Dijon mustard
1 tablespoon tarragon vinegar
2 teaspoons brown sugar
6 (2-ounce) unpeeled fresh apricots, cut into wedges

Directions

Press the spinach between paper towels to remove excess moisture.
Combine with the cottage cheese, bread crumbs, shallot, egg white, garlic
powder, nutmeg and salt in a bowl and mix well. Rinse the chicken and pat
dry. Spoon the spinach mixture onto the chicken and roll to enclose the filling;
secure with wooden picks. Chill in the refrigerator for 1 hour.

Brown the chicken rolls in the heated oil in a large skillet for 7 minutes
on each side. Remove chicken to a warm platter. Add the apricot nectar,
mustard, vinegar and brown sugar and mix well. Bring to a boil and reduce
the heat. Simmer for 7 minutes. Add the apricots. Simmer until the sauce
thickens to the desired consistency. Serve over the chicken.

Serves Six
Preparation Time: 20 minutes, plus chilling time
Cooking Time: 25 to 30 minutes

Chicken with Sun-Dried Tomato Sauce

Drying produces chewy, intensely-flavored tomatoes, which are sold either dry-packed or packed in oil. Dry-pack tomatoes are lower in calories, fat and cholesterol, but benefit from soaking in some liquid, such as the chicken broth suggested here, to rehydrate them.

Ingredients

1/4 cup dry-pack sun-dried tomatoes
1/2 cup chicken broth
2 whole boneless skinless chicken breasts
1/2 cup sliced fresh mushrooms
2 tablespoons chopped green onions
2 cloves of garlic, finely chopped
1 tablespoon vegetable oil
1/2 cup milk
2 teaspoons cornstarch
1/2 teaspoon dried basil or 2 teaspoons fresh basil

Directions

Combine the sun-dried tomatoes with the chicken broth in a bowl and let stand for 30 minutes. Cut the chicken breasts into halves, rinse and pat dry. Sauté the mushrooms, green onions and garlic in a nonstick skillet over medium heat for 3 minutes or until the mushrooms are tender; remove with a slotted spoon.

Add the oil and chicken to the skillet. Cook until browned on both sides. Add the tomato and broth mixture. Bring to a boil and reduce the heat. Simmer, covered, for 10 minutes, stirring occasionally. Remove the chicken to a warm platter.

Mix the milk, cornstarch and basil in a small bowl. Stir into the tomato mixture. Bring to a boil and boil for 1 minute, stirring constantly. Stir in the mushroom mixture. Cook until heated through. Serve over pasta or rice.

Serves Four
Preparation Time: 15 minutes, plus standing time
Cooking Time: 30 minutes

Versatile Baked Chicken

This basic recipe consists of eight chicken breasts, a butter mixture and a crumb mixture, with two variations. The same general directions apply for all three versions.

Ingredients

1 cup crushed sesame crackers
1 teaspoon garlic salt
$^1/_2$ teaspoon pepper
8 boneless skinless chicken breast halves
$^3/_4$ cup melted butter
1 tablespoon lemon juice

Directions

Mix the cracker crumbs, garlic salt and pepper together. Rinse the chicken and pat dry. Dip into a mixture of the butter and lemon juice and coat with the crumb mixture. Arrange in a 2-quart baking dish. Drizzle with any remaining butter mixture and sprinkle with any remaining crumb mixture. Bake at 350 degrees for 45 to 60 minutes or until cooked through.

Variation I: Combine $^1/_2$ cup melted butter and 2 minced cloves of garlic for the butter mixture. Combine $^1/_2$ cup Italian bread crumbs, $1^1/_2$ cups shredded Cheddar cheese, $^1/_4$ cup grated Parmesan cheese, 1 teaspoon salt and $^1/_2$ teaspoon pepper for the crumb mixture.

Variation II: Combine $^1/_2$ cup melted unsalted butter, 2 minced cloves of garlic, 1 teaspoon Worcestershire sauce and 1 teaspoon dry mustard for the butter mixture. Combine 2 cups bread crumbs, $^1/_2$ cup grated Parmesan cheese, $^1/_3$ cup chopped parsley and 1 (3-ounce) can French-fried onions for the crumb mixture.

Serves Eight
Preparation Time: 10 minutes
Cooking Time: 45 to 60 minutes

Turkey Enchiladas

This lean version of the Southwestern favorite is so tasty that family and guests will never miss the fat and cholesterol.

Ingredients

1 pound ground turkey
1 medium onion, chopped
1 (16-ounce) can dark red kidney beans
1 envelope burrito seasoning mix
1 (16-ounce) can enchilada sauce
$1/2$ to $3/4$ cup water
8 large flour tortillas
1 (12-ounce) jar picante sauce
$1/2$ to $3/4$ cup shredded Cheddar cheese
$1/2$ cup sour cream

Directions

Sauté the ground turkey in a large nonstick skillet until brown and crumbly. Add the onion and sauté for several minutes longer. Process the kidney beans in the food processor until smooth. Add to the turkey with the burrito seasoning mix, enchilada sauce and water and mix well. Simmer for 10 minutes.

Spoon the mixture onto the tortillas and roll to enclose the filling. Place seam side down on a baking sheet sprayed with nonstick cooking spray. Spoon the picante sauce over the top and sprinkle with the cheese. Bake at 350 degrees until heated through. Top with the sour cream to serve.

Serves Eight
Preparation Time: 20 minutes
Cooking Time: 30 minutes

Rock Cornish Game Hens with Wild Rice

*These miniature chickens are an American cross between Cornish
and White Rock or Plymouth Rock chickens and are best at a weight of
about 2 pounds. They usually serve just one person because of the
relatively small amount of meat to bone.*

Ingredients

3/4 cup uncooked wild rice
1 1/2 cups orange juice
1 or 2 medium onions, chopped
3/4 cup sliced mushrooms
4 Rock Cornish game hens
1 (6-ounce) can frozen orange juice concentrate, thawed
1/2 cup sherry
1/4 cup water

Directions

Rinse the rice. Add to 1 1/2 cups boiling orange juice in a saucepan. Bring
to a boil and reduce the heat. Simmer, covered, for 45 minutes or until tender.
Sauté the onions in a nonstick skillet over low heat until tender and light
brown. Add the mushrooms. Sauté over high heat for several minutes, adding
a drop or two of water if needed to prevent sticking. Drain the rice, reserving
any remaining cooking liquid. Combine the rice and mushroom mixture in
a bowl and mix well.

Rinse the hens inside and out, discarding the giblets, and pat dry. Stuff
with the rice mixture, spooning any remaining rice into a small baking dish.
Place the hens in a baking pan. Combine the reserved cooking liquid
with the orange juice concentrate, wine and water in a bowl and mix well.
Pour over the hens. Bake at 350 degrees for 1 1/2 hours. Bake the remaining
rice for 10 minutes or until heated through. Serve the cooking juices with the
hens and rice.

Serves Four
Preparation Time: 20 minutes
Cooking Time: 2 1/2 hours

Seafood and
Shellfish

Seafood and Shellfish

Flounder Florentine, 167
Broiled Grouper with Tomato and Herbs, 168
Cracker Crumb Fried Grouper, 168
Mahi Mahi Satay, 169
Mahi Mahi with Mango Salsa, 169
Baked Whole Red Snapper, 170
Red Snapper with Black Bean and Corn Salsa, 171
Salmon with Lemon and Dill Sauce, 172
Grilled Swordfish with Salsa Fresca, 173
Salsa Fresca, 173
Swordfish with Red Pepper Sauce, 174
Florida Yellowfin Tuna Ragout, 175
Crab Cakes, 176
Mrs. Thomas A. Edison's Deviled Crab, 177
Baked Lobster, 177
Scallops Oriental, 178
Scallops with Green Herbs, 178
Shrimp Bernese, 179
Shrimp Boil*, 180
Charleston–Style Shrimp Curry, 180
Jumbo Shrimp with Chive Butter, 181
Savory Shrimp, 181
Marinated Grilled Shrimp with Tarragon, 182
Shrimp Remoulade, 182

Seafood Pasta

Fusilli with Seafood Sauce, 183
Linguini with Clam and Shrimp Sauce, 184
Penne and Sun–Dried Tomatoes with Tuna, 184
Shrimp and Mushroom Fettuccini, 185
South Florida Seafood Pasta, 186
Spicy Basil and Scallop Linguini, 187
Spicy Lobster Pasta, 188

*Photograph Recipe

Flounder Florentine

Flounder, a member of the family that includes English sole, is a fine-textured fish with a delicate flavor. Other white fish could be substituted for the flounder in this recipe.

Ingredients

1 (10-ounce) package frozen chopped spinach
$1/2$ cup chopped onion
$1/2$ cup nonfat dry milk powder
$1^1/2$ cups chicken broth
$1/2$ cup flour
$1/2$ cup melted margarine or butter
1 cup shredded Swiss cheese
$1/3$ cup grated Parmesan cheese
$1/4$ cup dry white wine
1 ($2^1/2$-ounce) jar sliced mushrooms, drained
$1/2$ teaspoon salt
White pepper to taste
6 (4-ounce) flounder fillets
Juice of 1 lemon
Paprika to taste

Directions

Cook the spinach using the package directions and adding the onion; drain well. Dissolve the dry milk powder in the chicken broth in a bowl. Stir the flour into the melted margarine in a saucepan. Cook over low heat for 2 to 3 minutes. Stir in the milk mixture. Cook until thickened, stirring constantly; do not boil. Add the cheeses, wine, mushrooms, salt and white pepper.

Stir 1 cup of the sauce into the spinach. Sprinkle the fish with lemon juice. Spread the spinach mixture on the fillets. Roll the fish to enclose the filling and secure with wooden picks. Place seam side down in a shallow baking dish. Bake at 350 degrees for 15 minutes. Spoon the remaining sauce over the rolls and sprinkle with paprika. Bake for 20 to 25 minutes longer or until cooked through.

Serves Six
Preparation Time: 20 minutes
Cooking Time: 45 to 60 minutes

Broiled Grouper with Tomato and Herbs

You may double this recipe, but do not increase the amount of butter.

Ingredients

1/2 medium white onion, chopped
1 tablespoon butter   1 tomato, chopped
1 tablespoon chopped fresh basil
2 (4-ounce) grouper fillets or other white fish fillets
3 tablespoons fresh lemon juice
Salt and pepper to taste
2 tablespoons butter

Directions

Sauté the onion in 1 tablespoon butter in a small iron skillet. Add the tomato and basil and sauté for 2 to 3 minutes longer. Remove the tomato mixture with a slotted spoon. Sprinkle the fish with the lemon juice, salt and pepper. Sauté in 1 tablespoon butter in the skillet for 3 minutes on each side. Spoon the tomato mixture onto the fillets. Dot with the remaining tablespoon of butter. Broil until golden brown.

Serves Two
Preparation Time: 10 minutes
Cooking Time: 12 to 15 minutes

Cracker Crumb Fried Grouper

Choose the freshest catch of the day, such as grouper, flounder, redfish, snapper or snook for this dish.

Ingredients

1 egg, beaten
3 tablespoons water
6 small to medium grouper fillets
1/2 cup flour
24 to 30 butter crackers, coarsely crushed
Oil for frying

Directions

Beat the egg with the water in a bowl. Coat the fish with the flour and dip into the egg mixture. Coat with the cracker crumbs, pressing to cover well. Place on a plate in the freezer for 30 minutes. Fry in the oil until golden brown on both sides.

Serves Six
Preparation Time: 15 minutes, plus chilling time
Cooking Time: 10 minutes

Mahi Mahi Satay

*Satay or saté is an Indonesian favorite consisting
of small cubes of marinated meat, fish or poultry grilled,
typically served with a spicy peanut sauce.*

Ingredients

1 cup soy sauce or $1/2$ cup hoisin sauce and $1/2$ cup water
3 tablespoons smooth peanut butter
$1/2$ to 1 teaspoon red pepper flakes
$1^1/4$ pounds mahi mahi fillets, cut into $1^1/2$-inch pieces
1 cup dry-roasted peanuts, ground

Directions

Bring the soy sauce, peanut butter and red pepper to a boil in a small
saucepan. Cool for 10 to 15 minutes. Add the fish, turning to coat well.
Marinate for just 15 minutes; overmarinating causes the fish to become too
salty. Thread onto soaked bamboo skewers and roll in the peanuts, coating
well. Grill for 5 minutes, turning after 2 minutes. Serve over rice.

Serves Four
Preparation Time: 10 minutes, plus cooling and marinating time
Cooking Time: 10 minutes

Mahi Mahi with Mango Salsa

*Mahi mahi is a firm fish that is best prepared simply, as it is here.
The spicy salsa made from fresh mangos add interesting flavor.*

Ingredients

3 medium mangos, peeled, chopped
$1/4$ cup finely chopped red onion
$1/4$ cup finely chopped fresh cilantro or mint
Juice of 1 lime $1/3$ cup orange juice
3 jalapeño peppers, seeded, finely chopped
Salt and pepper to taste
2 (8-ounce) mahi mahi fillets

Directions

Combine the first 8 ingredients and mix well. Chill in the refrigerator.
Place the mahi mahi in a baking dish. Bake at 450 degrees for 10 minutes or
until the fish flakes easily. Serve with the mango salsa.

Serves Two
Preparation Time: 10 minutes, plus chilling time
Cooking Time: 10 minutes

Baked Whole Red Snapper

Your fishmonger may reduce the price per pound when you buy a whole fish. Ask him to remove the eyes, gills and scales before you take it home.

Ingredients

1 whole (3- to 4-pound) red snapper, cleaned
5 lemon slices, cut into halves
1/4 cup dry white wine
1/4 cup fresh orange juice
Juice of 1 lemon
3 tablespoons butter or margarine, softened
1 or 2 cloves of garlic, minced
1/2 teaspoon paprika
Salt and pepper to taste

Directions

Score the fish with 4 to 5 diagonal slashes on each side. Place the lemon slices in the slashes. Place the fish in a large baking dish and drizzle with the wine, orange juice and lemon juice. Spread the butter evenly over the fish and sprinkle with the garlic, paprika, salt and pepper.

Bake at 350 degrees for 35 minutes or until the fish flakes easily. Cut horizontally through the fish just above the skeleton, taking care not to disturb the skeleton and remove the fillet. Discard the skeleton. Replace the top fillet for a boneless presentation.

Serves Six
Preparation Time: 15 minutes
Cooking Time: 35 minutes

Red Snapper with Black Bean and Corn Salsa

This salsa adds a pleasant zest to the fish, which is fairly bland. Increase the amount of jalapeño pepper in the salsa to please the tastes of your family and guests.

Ingredients

1 cup drained black beans
1 cup fresh corn or thawed frozen corn
1 cup chopped red onion
1 medium green bell pepper, chopped
7 small radishes, chopped
3 tablespoons sherry vinegar or red wine vinegar
1 tablespoon lime juice
1/2 to 1 tablespoon minced jalapeño pepper with seeds
Salt and pepper to taste
4 (6-ounce) red snapper fillets
2 tablespoons olive oil

Directions

Combine the beans, corn, onion, bell pepper, radishes, vinegar, lime juice and jalapeño pepper in a bowl and mix well. Season with salt and pepper. Let stand, covered, at room temperature for 1 hour.

Brown the fish in the olive oil in a large heavy nonstick skillet for 3 minutes on each side. Remove to serving plates. Spoon the salsa over the fish.

Serves Four
Preparation Time: 20 minutes, plus standing time
Cooking Time: 6 minutes

Salmon with Lemon and Dill Sauce

Salmon should be broiled, poached or grilled for 10 minutes for each inch of thickness at its thickest point, turning halfway through the cooking time.

Ingredients

2 teaspoons cornstarch
$1/4$ cup lemon juice
$2/3$ cup water
2 teaspoons chopped fresh dill
2 teaspoons margarine
$1/2$ teaspoon grated lemon rind
$1/8$ teaspoon salt
Pepper to taste
2 pounds salmon fillets

Garnish

Sprigs of fresh dill

Directions

Blend the cornstarch and lemon juice in a saucepan. Add the water gradually. Cook over medium heat until thickened, stirring constantly. Remove from the heat and stir in the chopped dill, margarine, lemon rind, salt and pepper; keep warm.

Grill the salmon until it flakes easily. Serve with the dill sauce; garnish with dill sprigs.

Serves Six
Preparation Time: 5 minutes
Cooking Time: 15 minutes

Grilled Swordfish with Salsa Fresca

Swordfish is such a firm fish that it can be prepared in almost any manner, much as beef can be. It easily becomes too dry, however, in the cooking process, so moisture should be added in the form of marinade or butter.

Ingredients

4 swordfish steaks   1/2 cup olive oil
1/4 cup orange juice   2 tablespoons lime juice
1 tablespoon chopped parsley or cilantro
Salt and freshly ground pepper to taste
1 1/2 cups Salsa Fresca

Directions

Arrange the fish steaks in a single layer in a shallow dish. Combine the olive oil, orange juice, lime juice, parsley, salt and pepper in a bowl and mix well. Pour over the fish. Marinate, covered, in the refrigerator for 1 hour or longer; drain. Spray the grill with nonstick cooking spray. Grill the steaks for 5 minutes on each side or until they can be easily flaked. Serve with the Salsa Fresca.

Serves Four
Preparation Time: 10 minutes, plus marinating time
Cooking Time: 10 minutes

Salsa Fresca

This surprising salsa, with its combination of colorful fruits and vegetables, would be just as delicious with other grilled meats, fish or poultry.

Ingredients

2 red tomatoes, chopped   2 yellow tomatoes, chopped
1 bunch green onions, chopped   1 red onion, chopped
1 mango, chopped   1 cantaloupe, chopped
1 honeydew melon, chopped   1 bunch mint, chopped
Juice of 2 lemons   Juice of 2 limes
1 jalapeño pepper, chopped   1 1/2 tablespoons vegetable oil

Directions

Combine the tomatoes, green onions, red onion, mango, cantaloupe, honeydew, mint, lemon juice, lime juice, jalapeño pepper and oil in a bowl and mix well. Let stand for 2 hours or longer.

Yields Six Cups
Preparation Time: 15 minutes, plus standing time

Swordfish with Red Pepper Sauce

Tuna, halibut and other firm-fleshed fish can be substituted for the swordfish in this recipe. The red pepper flakes and Dijon mustard add a zip to the sweet red pepper in the sauce.

Ingredients

5 scallions, chopped
1 red bell pepper, chopped
2 cloves of garlic, minced
1 tablespoon olive oil
2 teaspoons paprika
1 teaspoon dried thyme leaves
1/8 teaspoon red pepper flakes
Salt and black pepper to taste
2 tablespoons Dijon mustard
1 or 2 fresh tomatoes, chopped
2 pounds swordfish steaks
1 tablespoon olive oil

Directions

Reserve 2 tablespoons of the scallions and red bell pepper. Sauté the garlic in 1 tablespoon olive oil in a small saucepan over low heat. Increase the heat to medium and add the remaining scallions, remaining red bell pepper, paprika, thyme, red pepper flakes, salt and black pepper. Sauté for 5 minutes. Stir in the mustard and tomatoes. Cook for 5 minutes longer; keep warm.

Brush the fish with 1 tablespoon olive oil. Grill for 3 to 4 minutes or just until cooked through. Top with the red pepper sauce; sprinkle with the reserved scallions and red bell pepper.

Serves Four
Preparation Time: 10 minutes
Cooking Time: 20 minutes

Florida Yellowfin Tuna Ragout

Save this dish for a cooler day, when cooking outside on the grill does not seem so attractive and the comfort of a ragout does.

Ingredients

1 cup sliced fresh mushrooms
1 cup diagonally sliced celery
3 carrots, julienned
1/2 cup chopped onion
1/4 cup chopped green bell pepper
1/4 cup chopped red bell pepper
1 clove of garlic, minced
2 tablespoons olive oil
1 (28-ounce) can tomatoes with no salt added
1 cup dry white wine
3/4 teaspoon sugar
1/4 teaspoon thyme
1/4 teaspoon sweet basil
Salt and pepper to taste
2 pounds yellowfin tuna steaks, cut into 1-inch cubes

Directions

Sauté the mushrooms, celery, carrots, onion, bell peppers and garlic in the oil in a saucepan. Add the tomatoes, wine, sugar, thyme, basil, salt and pepper. Simmer, covered, for 20 minutes.

Add the tuna. Simmer, covered, for 5 to 6 minutes or until the tuna is cooked through. Serve over rice or pasta.

Serves Eight
Preparation Time: 15 minutes
Cooking Time: 25 minutes

Crab Cakes

Blue crabs are the most common crab to Florida and the Gulf Coast. The lump or backfin meat from the body is the top grade of meat, followed by the smaller flake pieces from the body and claw meat.

Ingredients

1 small onion, chopped
1 medium green bell pepper, chopped
2 tablespoons olive oil
1 pound fresh backfin or lump crab meat
2 tablespoons mayonnaise
1 tablespoon mustard
1/2 cup fine Italian bread crumbs
2 eggs, beaten
1/2 teaspoon salt
1 teaspoon pepper

Directions

Sauté the onion and green pepper in the olive oil in a skillet until tender. Combine with the crab meat, mayonnaise, mustard, bread crumbs, eggs, salt and pepper in a bowl and mix gently; mixture will be thin.

Spoon into 6 mounds in a heated nonstick skillet; press slightly with a spatula. Cook over medium heat until golden brown on both sides; do not overcook. Serve immediately.

Serves Six
Preparation Time: 10 minutes
Cooking Time: 5 to 10 minutes

Mrs. Thomas A. Edison's Deviled Crab

The "devil" in this favorite dish of winter residents Mina and Thomas Edison is the dry mustard, Worcestershire sauce and red pepper. Prepare it in advance and add a crisp salad and crusty bread for a festive dinner.

Ingredients

1/3 cup butter, softened   1 tablespoon flour
1 teaspoon dry mustard   2 eggs
1 tablespoon Worcestershire sauce
1/2 cup finely chopped celery
1/2 teaspoon salt
Ground red pepper to taste
1/2 cup cream or evaporated skim milk
2 1/2 cups crab meat   1 cup bread crumbs
2 tablespoons melted butter

Directions

Cream the butter with the flour and dry mustard in a mixer bowl. Add the eggs, Worcestershire sauce, celery, salt, red pepper and cream and mix well. Fold in the crab meat. Spoon into 6 scallop shells; sprinkle with a mixture of the bread crumbs and melted butter. Bake at 350 degrees for 10 to 15 minutes or until light brown.

Serves Six
Preparation Time: 15 minutes
Cooking Time: 10 to 15 minutes

Baked Lobster

Lobster is so good that it needs nothing more than this simple preparation. Serve it with additional melted butter.

Ingredients

4 lobster tails   1/4 cup melted butter
Leaves of 1/2 head iceberg lettuce

Directions

Split the lobster tails down the back and fan open. Place in a roasting pan with 1/2 to 1 inch of water. Drizzle with the melted butter and cover completely with the lettuce leaves. Bake at 350 degrees for 20 minutes. Discard the lettuce leaves. Serve with additional melted butter.

Serves Four
Preparation Time: 10 minutes
Cooking Time: 20 minutes

Scallops Oriental

Calico scallops are the most common scallop found in the Gulf of Mexico and along the east coast of Florida. They are actually deep-sea creatures and are more plentiful than the true bay scallop found along the East Coast.

Ingredients

2 pounds scallops $1/4$ cup honey
$1/4$ cup prepared mustard
1 teaspoon lemon juice   2 teaspoons curry powder

Directions

Place the scallops in a broiler pan lined with foil. Combine the honey, mustard, lemon juice and curry powder in a bowl and mix well. Brush over the scallops. Broil far from the heat source for 10 minutes. Turn and broil until golden brown.

Serves Six
Preparation Time: 5 minutes
Cooking Time: 15 to 20 minutes

Scallops with Green Herbs

The delicate flavor of scallops is enhanced by the addition of the fresh herbs in this simple but elegant dish.

Ingredients

1 or 2 cloves of garlic, minced
$1/2$ cup unsalted butter   2 tablespoons chopped fresh dill
2 tablespoons chopped fresh parsley
2 tablespoons chopped green onions with tops
1 pound fresh sea scallops

Garnish

1 lemon, cut into wedges

Directions

Sauté the garlic in the butter in a skillet just until tender but not brown. Add the dill, parsley, green onions and scallops. Cook over medium heat for 3 to 4 minutes or until the scallops are cooked through, stirring frequently. Spoon onto a serving platter. Drizzle with the cooking juices. Garnish with lemon wedges.

Serves Four
Preparation Time: 10 minutes
Cooking Time: 8 minutes

Shrimp Bernese

The most important aspect of cooking shrimp is to know when to stop: shrimp is done when it is just pink. To arrest the cooking process and insure a nice texture, drain the shrimp immediately and cover it with ice cubes, draining the water as it accumulates.

Ingredients

3 pounds uncooked shrimp, peeled, deveined
Salt to taste
8 ounces fresh mushrooms or 2 (6-ounce) cans sliced mushrooms
$1/4$ cup butter
2 tomatoes, finely chopped
1 medium onion, grated
2 tablespoons flour
1 cup half-and-half
1 tablespoon Worcestershire sauce
$1/4$ cup sherry
$1/2$ teaspoon salt
$1/4$ teaspoon pepper
$3/4$ cup bread crumbs
$1 1/2$ tablespoons melted butter
$1/4$ teaspoon paprika

Directions

Cook the shrimp in salted water in a saucepan for 3 minutes; drain and cool. Peel and devein the shrimp. Chop the stems of the fresh mushrooms. Sauté the stems in $1/4$ cup butter in a skillet for 5 minutes. Slice the mushroom caps and add to the skillet. Sauté for 2 minutes. Add the tomatoes and onion. Cook over low heat for 10 minutes.

Blend the flour with the half-and-half in a bowl. Add the Worcestershire sauce, wine, $1/2$ teaspoon salt and pepper and mix well. Add to the mushroom mixture in the skillet. Cook for 10 to 15 minutes or until thickened, stirring constantly. Stir in the shrimp. Spoon into a baking dish. Top with a mixture of the bread crumbs and melted butter and sprinkle with the paprika. Bake at 350 degrees for 20 minutes; do not overcook.

Serves Eight
Preparation Time: 20 minutes
Cooking Time: 45 minutes

Shrimp Boil

For a true southwest Florida shrimp boil, replace the tablecloth with newspapers and serve it with plenty of cocktail sauce, lemon wedges, crackers and cold beer.

Ingredients

2 pounds kielbasa, cut into 2-inch lengths
1 medium onion, chopped   ¹/₄ cup shrimp seasoning
2 gallons (about) water   5 ears of corn, cut into halves
2 pounds whole new potatoes   3 pounds shrimp, peeled, deveined

Directions

Add the sausage, onion and shrimp seasoning to the boiling water in a very large saucepan. Return to a boil and add the corn and potatoes. Boil for 15 minutes. Add the shrimp. Cook for 4 to 5 minutes or until pink, stirring frequently; do not overcook; drain. Serve with butter or cocktail sauce.

Serves Ten
Preparation Time: 10 minutes
Cooking Time: 20 minutes

Charleston-Style Shrimp Curry

Serve this dish with flaked coconut, sliced bananas, toasted almonds, fig preserves, chutney, crumbled bacon and/or chopped hard-cooked egg.

Ingredients

3 pounds large shrimp   3 cups water
1 large onion, finely chopped   ¹/₂ cup finely chopped celery
¹/₂ cup finely chopped apple   ¹/₄ cup butter or margarine
1 cup water   2 cups heavy cream or half-and-half
2 tablespoons curry powder   ¹/₂ teaspoon salt
¹/₂ teaspoon pepper

Directions

Add the shrimp to 3 cups boiling water in a large saucepan. Return to a boil and reduce the heat. Simmer for 3 minutes; do not overcook. Drain and rinse with cold water; chill. Peel and devein the shrimp. Sauté the onion, celery and apple in the butter in a skillet for 5 minutes. Add 1 cup water. Simmer over low heat for 25 minutes or until most of the liquid has evaporated. Stir in the remaining ingredients. Simmer for 10 minutes, stirring occasionally. Add the shrimp and simmer until heated through. Serve over rice.

Serves Eight
Preparation Time: 45 minutes
Cooking Time: 45 minutes

Jumbo Shrimp with Chive Butter

*Jumbo shrimp have a count of 11 to 15 per pound and
are sometimes referred to as prawns in the United States. Just
six of these is enough for a serving.*

Ingredients

1/4 cup lemon juice
1/4 cup Dijon mustard
1 cup melted butter
6 tablespoons chopped fresh chives
Salt and freshly ground pepper to taste
36 uncooked jumbo shrimp

Directions

Whisk the lemon juice into the mustard in a bowl. Whisk in the butter
and chives gradually. Season with salt and pepper. Peel, devein and butterfly
the shrimp. Arrange cut side up on a broiler pan. Brush with some of the
butter mixture. Broil for 4 minutes or just until cooked through. Serve with
the remaining butter mixture.

Serves Six
Preparation Time: 15 minutes
Cooking Time: 4 minutes

Savory Shrimp

*Cooking shrimp in the shells, as it is here, adds considerable
flavor. They can be deveined either before or after cooking with
the point of a sharp knife.*

Ingredients

1 (16-ounce) bottle of Italian salad dressing
1 1/2 cups melted butter
1 lemon, sliced
1 3/4 ounces pepper, or to taste
5 pounds unpeeled shrimp

Directions

Combine the salad dressing, butter, lemon and pepper in a bowl. Add
the shrimp and mix well. Spoon into a baking dish. Bake for 45 to 60 minutes.
Serve in bowls with the cooking juices for dipping.

Serves Twelve
Preparation Time: 10 minutes
Cooking Time: 45 to 60 minutes

Marinated Grilled Shrimp with Tarragon

The aromatic anise flavor of tarragon has a natural affinity for shellfish marinades, but should be used sparingly.

Ingredients

1/4 cup vegetable oil   2 tablespoons lemon juice
2 tablespoons soy sauce   2 tablespoons dry sherry
2 teaspoons prepared mustard   2 teaspoons dried tarragon
2 teaspoons chopped fresh parsley
1/4 teaspoon freshly ground pepper   3 pounds medium shrimp

Directions

Mix the first 8 ingredients in a bowl. Peel the shrimp, leaving the tails intact. Add to the marinade, stirring to coat well. Marinate in the refrigerator for 2 hours. Drain, reserving the marinade. Arrange the shrimp on the rack in a broiler pan. Broil 3 inches from the heat source for 2 minutes. Turn and brush with the reserved marinade. Broil until cooked through.

Serves Eight
Preparation Time: 10 minutes, plus marinating time
Cooking Time: 5 minutes

Shrimp Rémoulade

Shrimp rémoulade brings all the flavor of New Orleans to your dinner table, to the delight of your guests.

Ingredients

1/2 cup sliced green onions   1/4 cup chopped celery
1 cup parsley   2 cloves of garlic
5 tablespoons Creole mustard or spicy brown mustard
1 tablespoon horseradish   Hot sauce to taste
2 tablespoons paprika   Salt and pepper to taste   1/3 cup vinegar
2/3 cup olive oil   1 pound shrimp, cooked, peeled, deveined

Directions

Process the green onions, celery, parsley and garlic in a blender or food processor until finely chopped. Combine with the mustard, horseradish, hot sauce, paprika, salt and pepper in a bowl and mix well. Stir in the vinegar, then the olive oil, gradually. Add the shrimp and mix well. Chill in the refrigerator for 3 hours or longer. Serve on a bed of shredded lettuce or pasta.

Serves Four
Preparation Time: 15 minutes, plus chilling time

Fusilli with Seafood Sauce

A general rule with pasta is that chunkier sauces go best with chunky pasta, so the fusilli is a good choice for this sauce with mussels and scallops. You can substitute shrimp for the mussels if you prefer.

Ingredients

1/2 cup dry white wine
1/4 cup water
1 large onion, thinly sliced
1/2 bay leaf
Salt to taste
2 black peppercorns
12 mussels or shrimp, scrubbed
1 (1-pound) bunch broccoli
2 tablespoons pine nuts (optional)
1/4 cup olive oil
8 ounces sea scallops, cut into halves or quarters
2 or 3 cloves of garlic, minced
1 (7-ounce) jar roasted red peppers, drained, finely chopped
8 ounces fusilli or spaghetti, cooked

Directions

Combine the wine, water, 2 onion slices, bay leaf, salt and peppercorns in a large skillet. Add the mussels. Bring to a boil, covered, over high heat. Reduce the heat and simmer for 3 to 4 minutes or until mussels open, shaking the skillet occasionally. Remove the mussels to a bowl, discarding the ones that fail to open. Strain the cooking liquid into a measuring cup. Add enough water, if necessary, to measure 3/4 cup. Cut the florets from the broccoli and sliced the stems into 1/4x2-inch strips.

Sauté the pine nuts in the heated olive oil in a large skillet until light brown. Remove with a slotted spoon to drain. Add the remaining onions slices and the broccoli stems. Sauté for 2 minutes. Add the broccoli florets, scallops and garlic. Sauté for 1 minute longer. Stir in the reserved cooking liquid and red peppers. Simmer, covered, over low heat for 2 to 3 minutes or until the scallops and broccoli are tender. Add the mussels. Cook until heated through.

Drain the pasta and place on a warm serving platter. Add the seafood sauce and toss to mix. Sprinkle with the pine nuts.

Serves Three
Preparation Time: 15 minutes
Cooking Time: 20 minutes

Linguini with Clam and Shrimp Sauce

*Except for the shrimp, this tempting dish can be ready in minutes
from items in your pantry. It needs only a salad of greens and a
crusty bread for a complete meal.*

Ingredients

1 pound medium shrimp, peeled, deveined
2 cloves of garlic, minced   2 tablespoons corn oil
1 (7-ounce) can chopped clams   2 tablespoons dried parsley flakes
1/2 cup dry white wine   1/2 teaspoon salt
1 tablespoon crushed red pepper
8 ounces linguini, cooked, drained

Directions

Sauté the shrimp and garlic in the heated oil in a large skillet over medium
heat for 1 to 2 minutes. Add the undrained clams, parsley, wine, salt and red
pepper. Simmer for 8 to 10 minutes. Serve over the linguini.

Serves Four
Preparation Time: 15 minutes
Cooking Time: 10 minutes

Penne and Sun-Dried Tomatoes with Tuna

*You will be the "catch of the day" when you serve this delicious pasta
dish bursting with the flavors of the Mediterranean.*

Ingredients

1/2 cup sun-dried tomatoes   2 tablespoons olive oil
4 cloves of garlic, minced
1 to 2 pounds fresh tuna, cut into bite-sized pieces
24 kalamata olives, cut into quarters   1/3 cup capers
1 (28-ounce) can crushed tomatoes   Salt and pepper to taste
16 ounces penne, cooked, drained   1/4 cup grated Parmesan cheese

Directions

Combine the sun-dried tomatoes with the olive oil in a bowl for 15
minutes. Drain the olive oil into a skillet and add the garlic. Sauté for 1 to 2
minutes. Add the sun-dried tomatoes, tuna, olives and capers. Cook until the
tuna is cooked through. Add the canned tomatoes, salt and pepper. Simmer
over low to medium heat until heated through. Spoon over the pasta in a large
serving bowl and toss to mix well. Sprinkle with the cheese.

Serves Eight
Preparation Time: 15 minutes
Cooking Time: 10 to 12 minutes

Shrimp and Mushroom Fettuccini

The expression al dente *means firm to the bite and is the best way to serve pasta, as overcooked pasta becomes a soft and sticky mass. If the pasta is to be cooked longer after the dish is assembled, it should be undercooked in the first step.*

Ingredients

6 to 8 cloves of garlic, finely chopped
$1/2$ cup butter
2 tablespoons sherry (optional)
1 pound fresh shrimp, peeled, deveined
8 ounces fresh mushrooms, sliced
1 pound fettuccini, cooked *al dente*
2 egg yolks
2 cups heavy cream
$1/4$ cup grated Parmesan cheese (optional)
Salt and pepper to taste

Directions

Cook the garlic in a mixture of the butter and sherry in a 10 to 12-inch skillet over medium heat until tender but not brown. Add the shrimp and mushrooms. Cook until the shrimp are firm and just pink. Add the pasta and cook until heated through, tossing lightly.

Beat the egg yolks and cream in a bowl. Add to the pasta and toss to mix well. Remove from the heat and sprinkle with the cheese, salt and pepper. Serve immediately.

Serves Four
Preparation Time: 10 minutes
Cooking Time: 15 minutes

South Florida Seafood Pasta

Enjoy this Florida combination of two of the most popular trends in today's cooking: seafood and pasta. You can vary the seafood, using the freshest available in your market.

Ingredients

1 pound uncooked linguini
2 tablespoons butter or margarine
Salt to taste
4 ounces fresh mussel meat
6 ounces fresh clams, chopped, cooked, drained
10 ounces fresh scallops
12 ounces fresh shrimp, peeled
1/4 cup olive oil
1/4 cup dry white wine
2 cups heavy cream
8 cloves of garlic, finely chopped
Pepper to taste

Directions

Cook the pasta *al dente* with the butter in salted water in a saucepan. Combine the mussel meat, clams, scallops and shrimp in a bowl and drain well.

Bring the olive oil, wine, cream, garlic, salt and pepper to a boil in a saucepan. Add the seafood and pasta and mix well. Cook over medium heat for 10 minutes or until the seafood is cooked through and the sauce if creamy. Serve immediately.

Serves Six
Preparation Time: 10 minutes
Cooking Time: 20 minutes

Spicy Basil and Scallop Linguini

Add delicate scallops to this red sauce reminiscent of the traditional sauces of the south of Italy for a dish sure to please.

Ingredients

2 shallots, minced
2 cloves of garlic, crushed
1 tablespoon olive oil
2 tablespoons minced Italian parsley
2 tablespoons finely chopped fresh basil
1 (16-ounce) can tomatoes
2 tablespoons tomato paste
$1/2$ cup dry white wine
$1/4$ teaspoon salt
$1/4$ teaspoon black pepper
$1/4$ tablespoon crushed red pepper
1 pound sea scallops
8 ounces linguini, cooked, drained

Directions

Sauté the shallots and garlic in the olive oil in a saucepan for 3 minutes. Add the parsley, basil, tomatoes, tomato paste, wine, salt, black pepper and crushed red pepper. Bring to a boil, stirring to break up the tomatoes.

Simmer, covered, for 20 minutes. Add the scallops. Cook for 15 minutes or until the scallops are cooked through. Add the pasta and toss to coat well.

Serves Six
Preparation Time: 10 minutes
Cooking Time: 40 to 45 minutes

Spicy Lobster Pasta

It doesn't take a lot of lobster for this delicious dish that will satisfy your taste in a more economical way.

Ingredients

3 medium lobster tails
2 tablespoons blackening spice
1 tablespoon vegetable oil
$^1/_2$ cup chopped peeled tomato
1 cup chopped fresh mushrooms
$^1/_3$ cup chopped leeks
$^1/_4$ cup chopped green onions
2 tablespoons minced garlic
1 ounce brandy
$^3/_4$ to 1 cup heavy cream
2 tablespoons *fines herbes*
12 ounces angel hair pasta, cooked

Directions

Remove the lobster meat from the shells and chop. Coat well with the blackening spice. Sauté in the oil in a skillet for 3 to 5 minutes or until cooked through. Remove the lobster with a slotted spoon. Add the tomato, mushrooms, leeks, green onions and garlic. Sauté until tender. Remove the vegetables from the skillet.

Add the brandy, stirring to deglaze. Cook for 1 minute. Stir in the cream, lobster and *fines herbes*. Cook for 3 to 5 minutes or until thickened to desired consistency. Combine the sauce with the pasta and vegetables in a serving bowl; toss to coat well. Serve immediately.

Serves Four
Preparation Time: 15 minutes.
Cooking Time: 8 to 12 minutes

Desserts

*Photograph Recipes

Bread Pudding with Whiskey Sauce

This pudding is made with French bread, but you can add variety by using raisin bread, crescent rolls or other breads.

For the whiskey sauce

1/2 cup butter, softened
1 cup sugar
1 egg
1/4 cup (about) whiskey

For the pudding

1 loaf stale French bread, sliced
1 quart milk
3 eggs
2 cups sugar
2 tablespoons vanilla extract
1 cup raisins
3 tablespoons margarine, melted

To prepare the whiskey sauce

Cream the butter and sugar in a double boiler until light and fluffy. Cook until the sugar dissolves and the mixture is very hot. Beat a small amount into the egg and beat the egg into the hot mixture. Cool to room temperature. Stir in the whiskey.

To prepare the pudding

Add the bread to the milk in a bowl and mix well with hands. Add the eggs, sugar, vanilla and raisins and mix well. Spread the margarine in a baking dish. Add the pudding mixture. Bake at 350 degrees for 1 hour or until firm; cool. Spoon into individual dessert dishes. Top with the whiskey sauce. Broil until bubbly.

Serves Eight
Preparation Time: 15 minutes
Cooking Time: 1 1/4 hours

Baked Apples

Much more than the name implies, these apples are chopped and baked in a wrapping of phyllo for a delicious dessert that is low in fat and calories.

Ingredients

4 medium apples, peeled, chopped   2 tablespoons honey
1 teaspoon cinnamon   1 tablespoon chopped mint
10 sheets frozen phyllo dough, thawed

Directions

Combine the apples with the honey, cinnamon and mint in a bowl and mix well. Stack the pastry sheets on a work surface and cut into eight 3x3-inch squares. Spray lightly with nonstick cooking spray. Spoon the apple mixture into the centers of the squares and bring the corners up to enclose the filling; twist and pinch to seal. Place on a baking sheet sprayed with nonstick cooking spray. Bake at 325 degrees for 15 minutes or until golden brown. Serve with frozen nonfat vanilla yogurt.

Serves Eight
Preparation Time: 15 minutes
Cooking Time: 15 minutes

Chocolate Decadence

The water bath used here is designed to surround the dish with gentle even heat in order to cook delicate mixtures without breaking, curdling or scorching them.

Ingredients

1 pound good quality semisweet chocolate
1 pound unsalted butter   6 eggs

Directions

Melt the chocolate and butter in a double boiler. Spoon into a bowl. Wash the double boiler and add the eggs to it. Cook the eggs over warm water just until heated through, whisking constantly; remove from the heat. Beat at high speed for 6 minutes or until thick and lemon-colored. Fold into the chocolate mixture $1/4$ at a time. Spoon into a springform pan and place in a water bath with 1 inch of water. Bake at 425 degrees for 15 minutes or until set. Cool on a wire rack for 1 hour. Chill for 24 hours. Place on a serving plate and remove the side of the pan. Serve topped with fresh fruit.

Serves Twelve
Preparation Time: 15 minutes, plus cooling and chilling time
Cooking Time: $1^{1}/_{4}$ hours

Chocolate Orange Mousse

Just like other beans, cocoa beans are a good source of protein, carbohydrates, fiber, vitamin B, phosphorus, iron and potassium. Cocoa butter, or the "fat" in cocoa beans, has no cholesterol, but it rates second only to coconut oil in the level of saturated fat.

Ingredients

1/2 teaspoon grated orange rind
2 teaspoons light brown sugar
1 egg yolk
1 egg
3 ounces semisweet chocolate, melted, cooled
1 1/2 teaspoons orange juice
1/2 cup whipping cream

Directions

Combine the orange rind, brown sugar, egg yolk and egg in a blender or food processor and process until light and foamy. Add the melted chocolate, orange juice and whipping cream; process until smooth.

Spoon into individual dessert dishes. Chill for 1 hour or until set.

Serves Two
Preparation Time: 10 minutes, plus chilling time

Cream-Filled Éclairs

*A cream puff becomes an éclair when a sweet frosting is
added. This one is filled with a vanilla pudding mixture, but you
could use the filling of your choice.*

For the filling

1 envelope whipped topping mix
1/2 cup milk
1 (3-ounce) package vanilla instant pudding mix
2 cups milk

For the éclairs

1 cup water
1/2 cup butter or margarine
1 cup flour, sifted
1/2 teaspoon salt
4 eggs
1 can chocolate frosting

To prepare the filling

Prepare the whipped topping mix according to the package directions,
using 1/2 cup milk. Prepare the pudding mix according to the package
directions, using 2 cups milk. Fold the whipped topping into the pudding.
Chill until thickened.

To prepare the éclairs

Bring the water to a boil in a saucepan. Stir in the butter until melted.
Add the flour and salt all at once, stirring to mix well. Cook over low heat
until the mixture leaves the side of the pan, stirring constantly. Cool for 1
minute. Beat in the eggs 1 at a time with a wooden spoon. Shape into
3/4x4-inch éclairs on a baking sheet. Bake at 450 degrees for 10 minutes.
Reduce the oven temperature to 400 degrees. Bake for 15 to 20 minutes longer
or until puffed and golden brown. Cool on a wire rack. Cut off the tops and
set aside. Fill with the pudding mixture and replace the tops. Top with the
chocolate frosting.

Serves Thirty
Preparation Time: 15 minutes, plus chilling time
Cooking Time: 40 minutes

Pavlova

*Pavlova is a famous meringue-based dessert named after the
Russian ballerina, Anna Pavlova. It was created in honor of her
performance of the dying swan in Swan Lake during her tour
of Australia and has become the "apple pie" of Australia.*

Ingredients

4 egg whites
1 cup sugar
1 teaspoon malt vinegar or white vinegar
$^1/_2$ teaspoon vanilla extract
2 cups whipping cream
2 bananas
2 tablespoons lemon juice
1 pint strawberries, cut into halves
2 kiwifruit, thinly sliced
1 passion fruit

Directions

Line a 7x11-inch baking pan with baking parchment, allowing the
parchment to extend above the sides. Grease the parchment and dust lightly
with flour. Beat the egg whites until soft peaks form. Add the sugar gradually,
beating after each addition until the sugar is completely dissolved. Add the
vinegar and vanilla and beat for 1 minute longer or until stiff. Spread in the
prepared baking dish.

Bake at 250 degrees for 45 minutes or until the surface of the meringue
is firm. Lift with the parchment to a wire rack to cool; the center will fall
slightly. Remove the parchment and trim the edges with a sharp knife.

Beat half the whipping cream in a mixer bowl until soft peaks form.
Spread over the cooled meringue. Slice the bananas diagonally and dip into
the lemon juice to prevent discoloration. Arrange the bananas, strawberries
and kiwifruit in a decorative pattern on the meringue. Remove the pulp
from the passion fruit and spoon over the bananas. Beat the remaining
whipping cream in a mixer bowl until soft peaks form. Pipe around the edge
of the Pavlova.

Serves Six
Preparation Time: 45 minutes
Cooking Time: 45 minutes

Cherry Champagne Ice

*For a really spectacular presentation for this light summer ice,
melt 1/3 cup semisweet or milk chocolate chips with 1 tablespoon of
shortening and pipe it into a decorative design on the inside
of the chilled dessert glasses before adding the ice.*

Ingredients

2/3 cup sugar
1/2 cup unsweetened cherry juice or white grape juice
2 1/2 cups pitted fresh tart red cherries or 1 (16-ounce) package
frozen unsweetened pitted tart cherries, slightly thawed
2/3 cup Champagne
1/2 teaspoon finely grated lemon rind

Garnish

Fresh mint sprigs

Directions

Combine the sugar and cherry juice in a medium saucepan. Cook over medium-high just until the sugar dissolves, stirring constantly. Let stand, covered, until cool.

Combine the cherries, Champagne and lemon rind in a blender or food processor container and process until nearly smooth. Stir into the cooled syrup. Pour into a 1 to 2-quart ice cream freezer and freeze using the manufacturer's directions. Scoop into dessert glasses piped with chocolate and garnish with mint.

Serves Four
Preparation Time: 15 minutes, plus freezing time
Cooking Time: 5 minutes

Mango Sherbet

The beautiful yellow color of this sherbet is as memorable as its tangy tropical flavor. It is delicious alone or with chocolate sauce.

Ingredients

1 1/3 cups fresh mango purée
1 cup buttermilk
1 cup sugar
2/3 cup water
Juice of 1 large lime

Directions

Combine the mango purée, buttermilk, sugar, water and lime juice in a bowl and mix well. Spoon into an ice cream freezer and freeze using the manufacturer's directions.

Serves Six
Preparation Time: 10 minutes, plus freezing time

Low-Fat Raspberry Cheesecake Parfaits

Don't be surprised if your guests ask for this recipe, but they will be surprised to discover how low in fat it is.

Ingredients

1/4 cup light ricotta cheese
1/4 cup nonfat cream cheese, softened
2 tablespoons sugar
1 cup fresh raspberries
2 tablespoons all-fruit raspberry spread
8 to 10 vanilla wafers, crushed
1/4 cup reduced-calorie whipped topping

Directions

Combine the ricotta cheese, cream cheese and sugar in a blender or food processor and process until smooth. Reserve 8 raspberries for topping. Combine the remaining raspberries and raspberry spread in a bowl and mix gently. Layer the raspberries, cheese mixture and cookie crumbs in 4 parfait glasses. Top with the reserved raspberries and the whipped topping. Chill for 2 hours.

Serves Four
Preparation Time: 10 minutes, plus chilling time

Orange Cream in Orange Cups

Nothing says "Florida" better than fresh oranges, and you are sure to enjoy this way to serve them.

Ingredients

8 juice oranges
1/2 cup (about) orange juice (optional)
1 cup sugar
1/4 cup brandy
2 envelopes unflavored gelatin
1/2 cup cold water
3 1/2 cups whipped cream

Garnish

Shaved chocolate

Directions

Cut off the tops of the oranges and scoop out the pulp, reserving the cups. Squeeze or process the pulp to yield 3 cups juice, adding additional juice if needed. Strain into a bowl and add the sugar and brandy, mixing well.

Soften the gelatin in the cold water in a double boiler. Heat over simmering water until the gelatin dissolves. Add to the orange juice very gradually, stirring constantly. Chill until the mixture mounds slightly. Fold in 2 cups whipped cream. Spoon into the reserved orange shells. Chill until set. Top with the remaining whipped cream. Garnish with the shaved chocolate.

Serves Eight
Preparation Time: 20 minutes, plus chilling time
Cooking Time: 5 minutes

Strawberries with Grand Marnier

In the sixteenth century, author William Butler wrote, "Doubtless God could have made a better berry, but doubtless God never did." He would doubtless have approved of this simple way to enjoy them.

Ingredients

1 pint fresh strawberries   2 ounces Grand Marnier
1 cup whipping cream   1 ounce Frangelico
1/4 to 1/2 cup confectioners' sugar

Directions

Chill a mixer bowl and beaters in the freezer for 20 minutes. Wash, drain, stem and quarter the strawberries. Combine with the Grand Marnier in a medium bowl and toss lightly. Chill, covered, in the refrigerator. Whip the cream in the chilled bowl until soft peaks form. Fold in the Frangelico and confectioners' sugar and beat until smooth. Spoon the strawberries into fluted champagne glasses and top with the whipped cream.

Serves Four
Preparation Time: 15 minutes, plus chilling time

Tropical Sundaes

This is an easy and colorful finish to a Southwest Florida seafood dinner. For a special presentation, serve the sundaes in an edible bowl of chocolate pastry or waffle cone bowls.

Ingredients

2 mangos or papayas, peeled, coarsely chopped
1 tablespoon maple syrup (optional)   1 star fruit, sliced
2 cups fresh pineapple cubes   1 cup thinly sliced papaya
1 cup strawberry halves   1 cup sliced bananas
2 plums, thinly sliced

Garnish

Fresh mint leaves

Directions

Purée the mangos in a blender or food processor until smooth. Press through a strainer into a bowl. Stir in the maple syrup. Arrange the remaining fruit in a decorative pattern on 4 dessert plates. Drizzle with the mango purée. Garnish with mint.

Serves Four
Preparation Time: 15 minutes

White Chocolate Mousse with Frangelico

Enjoy this sumptuous combination of white chocolate and hazelnut liqueur, topped with a dusting of cocoa for a striking color contrast.

Ingredients

8 ounces high-quality white chocolate, broken into small pieces
1/2 cup unsalted butter
6 egg yolks, at room temperature
1 cup sifted confectioners' sugar
1/2 cup Frangelico
6 egg whites, at room temperature
1/4 teaspoon cream of tartar
2 cups whipping cream, chilled, whipped

Garnish

Unsweetened baking cocoa or grated dark chocolate

Directions

Melt the white chocolate with the butter in a small saucepan, stirring to mix well. Beat the egg yolks, confectioners' sugar and liqueur in a mixer bowl until thick and lemon-colored. Pour into a double boiler. Cook over simmering water for 3 minutes or until very thick, whisking constantly. Spoon into a large bowl. Whisk in the white chocolate mixture.

Beat the egg whites with the cream of tartar in a bowl until stiff but not dry. Fold the egg whites and the whipped cream gently into the mousse. Chill, covered, for 3 hours or until firm. Spoon into individual dessert glasses. Garnish with cocoa or grated chocolate.

Serves Twelve
Preparation Time: 20 minutes, plus chilling time
Cooking Time: 3 minutes

Blueberry Cake

Serve this beautiful dessert with the whipped cream as suggested here, or omit the whipped cream for a delicious breakfast or brunch treat.

Ingredients

1/2 cup butter or margarine, softened
1/2 cup sugar
1 egg
1 1/2 cups flour
1 1/2 teaspoons baking powder
1 teaspoon vanilla extract
3 1/2 cups fresh blueberries
16 ounces sour cream
2 egg yolks
1/2 cup sugar
1 teaspoon vanilla extract
1 1/2 cups whipping cream
3/4 cup sifted confectioners' sugar

Garnish

Blueberries

Directions

Cream the butter in a mixer bowl until light. Add 1/2 cup sugar gradually, beating at medium speed until fluffy. Beat in the egg. Combine the flour and baking powder. Add to the creamed mixture and mix just until moistened. Stir in 1 teaspoon vanilla. Spoon into a 9-inch springform pan. Sprinkle with the blueberries.

Combine the sour cream, egg yolks, 1/2 cup sugar and 1 teaspoon vanilla in a bowl and mix well. Spoon over the batter in the pan. Bake at 350 degrees for 1 hour or until the edges are light brown. Cool in the pan on a wire rack. Chill, covered, in the refrigerator. Place on a serving plate and remove the side of the pan.

Beat the whipping cream in a mixer bowl until soft peaks begin to form. Add the confectioners' sugar gradually, beating constantly. Spoon half the whipped cream over the cake. Pipe the remaining whipped cream around the edge. Garnish with additional blueberries.

Serves Eight
Preparation Time: 30 minutes, plus chilling time
Cooking Time: 1 hour

Toasted Coconut Cake

*Nothing is better than fresh coconut, but few of us want
the trouble involved. The availability of frozen coconut, which is
the nearest thing to fresh coconut, makes this dessert just as
good as the one your grandmother used to make.*

For the cake

1 (2-layer) package yellow cake mix
1 (4-ounce) package vanilla instant pudding mix
1^1/$_3$ cups water
4 eggs
^{1}/$_4$ cup vegetable oil
2 cups coconut
1 cup chopped pecans

For the frosting

2 tablespoons butter or margarine
2 cups coconut
8 ounces cream cheese, softened
2 tablespoons butter or margarine, softened
2 tablespoons milk
3^1/$_2$ cups confectioners' sugar, sifted
^{1}/$_2$ teaspoon vanilla extract

To prepare the cake

Combine the cake mix, pudding mix, water, eggs and oil in a large mixer
bowl and beat at medium speed for 4 minutes. Stir in the coconut and pecans.
Spoon into 3 greased and floured 9-inch cake pans. Bake at 350 degrees for
35 minutes. Cool in the pans for 10 minutes and remove to a wire rack to
cool completely.

To prepare the frosting and frost the cake

Melt 2 tablespoons butter in a skillet and stir in the coconut. Cook over
low heat until toasted to a golden brown. Spread on paper towels to cool.
Beat the cream cheese with 2 tablespoons butter in a mixer bowl until
light. Add the milk and beat until smooth. Beat in the confectioners' sugar
gradually. Add the vanilla; mix well. Stir in 1^3/$_4$ cups of the coconut. Spread
between the layers and over the top and side of the cake. Sprinkle with the
remaining coconut.

Serves Sixteen
Preparation Time: 20 minutes, plus cooling time
Cooking Time: 35 minutes

Glazed Fudge Cake

This special cake with the style of a French gâteau takes a little more time than some, but the response it gets will reassure you that it is worth it.

For the cake

3/4 cup plus 2 tablespoons cake flour
1/3 cup blanched almonds, ground
1 teaspoon baking powder
1/2 teaspoon baking soda   1/2 teaspoon salt
2 (1-ounce) squares unsweetened chocolate, broken
1/4 cup sugar
1 tablespoon baking cocoa
1/3 cup boiling water   2 eggs   1 cup sugar
3/4 cup unsalted butter, cut into 6 pieces
1/2 cup sour cream
1 tablespoon dark rum

For the glaze

3 (1-ounce) squares semisweet chocolate
1 1/2 tablespoons dark rum
6 tablespoons unsalted butter, softened

Garnish

Almonds

To prepare the cake

Line the bottom of an 8 or 8 1/2-inch springform pan with baking parchment. Butter the parchment and the side of the pan. Combine the flour, almonds, baking powder, baking soda and salt in a food processor and process for 5 seconds. Place in a bowl. Combine the chocolate, 1/4 cup sugar and the cocoa in the food processor and process for 1 minute or until the chocolate is finely chopped. Add the boiling water, processing constantly until the chocolate melts. Add the eggs and process for 1 minute. Add 1 cup sugar and process for 1 minute, scraping the side of the bowl several times. Add the butter and process for 1 minute. Add the sour cream and rum and process for 5 seconds. Add the flour mixture and pulse several times or just until the flour is moistened; do not overmix. Spread evenly in the prepared pan. Bake at 325 degrees for 50 to 55 minutes or until the cake pulls from the side of the pan. Cool in the pan on a wire rack. Remove to a serving plate.

To prepare the glaze and finish the cake

Melt the chocolate in the rum in a saucepan. Beat in the butter. Cool until glaze if of spreading consistency. Spread over the side of the cake and then over the top. Garnish with almonds.

Serves Eight
Preparation Time: 30 minutes, plus cooling time
Cooking Time: 1 hour

Hot Fudge Pudding Cake

Serve this warm with a sprinkle of Kahlúa for a dessert that may not be on your diet, but will certainly be good for your soul.

Ingredients

3/4 cup sugar
1 cup flour
3 tablespoons baking cocoa
2 teaspoons baking powder
1/4 teaspoon salt
1/4 cup milk
1/3 cup melted butter or margarine
1 1/2 teaspoons vanilla extract
1/2 cup sugar
1/2 cup packed light brown sugar
1/4 cup baking cocoa
1 1/4 cups hot water

Directions

Mix 3/4 cup sugar, flour, 3 tablespoons cocoa, baking powder and salt in a medium mixer bowl. Add the milk, butter and vanilla and mix until smooth. Spoon into a square baking pan. Mix 1/2 cup sugar, brown sugar and 1/4 cup cocoa in a small bowl. Sprinkle over the batter and pour the hot water over the top; do not stir.

Bake at 350 degrees for 40 minutes or until the center is nearly set. Let stand for 15 minutes. Spoon the cake portion into serving dishes and spoon the sauce in the bottom of the pan over the top.

Serves Nine
Preparation Time: 15 minutes, plus standing time
Cooking Time: 40 minutes

Mango Cake

Floridians have a distinct advantage in enjoying local tree-ripened mangos, for, like most tropical fruits, mangos are much sweeter when they ripen on the tree.

For the cake

2^1/$_2$ cups mashed mangos
2 cups flour
2 cups sugar
2 teaspoons baking soda
2 eggs
1 teaspoon vanilla extract
1 cup chopped walnuts (optional)

For the frosting

8 ounces cream cheese, softened
^{1}/$_2$ cup butter or margarine, softened
2 teaspoons vanilla extract
^{3}/$_4$ cup confectioners' sugar

To prepare the cake

Combine the mangos, flour, sugar, baking soda, eggs and vanilla in a mixer bowl and beat until smooth. Stir in the walnuts. Spoon into a greased 9x13-inch baking pan. Bake at 350 degrees for 40 minutes. Cool on a wire rack.

To prepare the frosting and frost the cake

Beat the cream cheese, butter and vanilla in a mixer bowl until light. Add the confectioners' sugar, beating until smooth. Spread over the cake.

Serves Fifteen
Preparation Time: 20 minutes, plus cooling time
Cooking Time: 40 minutes

Pineapple and Carrot Cake

*Choose thinner carrots to use in a carrot cake, because the
thinner carrots are sweeter than the thicker ones.*

For the cake

3 cups flour
2 cups sugar
2 teaspoons baking powder
2 teaspoons baking soda
2 teaspoons cinnamon
1 teaspoon salt
1 1/2 cups vegetable oil
4 eggs
2 cups shredded carrots
1 (8-ounce) can crushed pineapple

For the frosting

8 ounces cream cheese, softened
1/2 cup butter or margarine, softened
3 tablespoons milk
2 teaspoons vanilla extract
5 cups confectioners' sugar
3/4 cup chopped pecans

To prepare the cake

Combine the flour, sugar, baking powder, baking soda, cinnamon and
salt in a mixer bowl. Add the oil, eggs, carrots and undrained pineapple and
mix well. Spoon into 3 greased and floured cake pans. Bake at 350 degrees
for 35 minutes or until the layers test done. Cool in the pans for 10 minutes
and remove to a wire rack to cool completely.

To prepare the frosting and frost the cake

Beat the cream cheese and butter in a mixer bowl until light. Beat in
the milk, vanilla and confectioners' sugar. Spread between the layers and over
the top of the cake, sprinkling each layer with pecans.

Serves Sixteen
Preparation Time: 20 minutes, plus cooling time
Cooking Time: 35 minutes

White Chocolate Cake

This cake is better if allowed to stand for a day or two before serving, but you may have to hide it to accomplish that.

For the cake

1 cup butter, softened
2 cups sugar
4 egg yolks
4 ounces white chocolate, melted, cooled
1 teaspoon vanilla extract
2$^1/_2$ cups sifted cake flour
1 teaspoon baking soda
$^1/_2$ teaspoon salt
1 cup buttermilk
4 egg whites, stiffly beaten
1 cup pecans
1 cup flaked coconut

For the frosting

1 cup evaporated milk
1 cup sugar
3 egg yolks
$^1/_2$ cup butter
1 teaspoon vanilla extract
1$^1/_3$ cups flaked coconut
1 cup chopped pecans

To prepare the cake

Cream the butter and sugar in a mixer bowl until light and fluffy. Beat in the egg yolks 1 at a time. Add the melted white chocolate and vanilla and mix well. Sift the flour, baking soda and salt together. Add to the creamed mixture alternately with the buttermilk, mixing well after each addition. Fold in the egg whites, pecans and coconut. Spoon into three 8 or 9-inch cake pans lined on the bottom with waxed paper. Bake at 350 degrees for 30 to 40 minutes or until the cake tests done. Cool in the pans for 10 minutes and remove to a wire rack to cool completely.

To prepare the frosting and frost the cake

Combine the evaporated milk, sugar, egg yolks, butter and vanilla in a saucepan. Cook over medium heat for 12 minutes or until thickened, stirring constantly. Stir in the coconut and pecans. Beat until of spreading consistency. Spread between the layers and over the top of the cake.

Serves Sixteen
Preparation Time: 30 minutes, plus cooling time
Cooking Time: 1 hour

Pecan Pralines

Share the flavor of the Vieux Carré in New Orleans with these pralines from your own kitchen.

Ingredients

1 cup sugar
2 cups packed brown sugar
1 cup whipping cream
1 cup water
3 cups pecans

Directions

Combine the sugar, brown sugar, cream and water in a saucepan and mix well. Cook to 238 degrees on the candy thermometer, soft-ball stage. Remove from the heat and beat until smooth and creamy. Stir in the pecans. Drop by spoonfuls onto buttered waxed paper. Let stand until firm.

Serves Thirty-Six
Preparation Time: 10 minutes
Cooking Time: 30 minutes

No-Bake Citrus Bites

These easy treats with the flavor of Florida are a welcome gift during the holidays and good to keep on hand the rest of the year.

Ingredients

$1/4$ cup margarine, softened
$1/2$ (16-ounce) package confectioners' sugar
8 ounces vanilla wafers, finely crushed
3 ounces thawed frozen orange juice concentrate
$1/2$ cup chopped pecans
$1/2$ cup flaked coconut

Directions

Cream the margarine and confectioners' sugar in a mixer bowl until light. Add the cookie crumbs, orange juice concentrate and pecans and mix well. Chill for 1 hour. Shape into bite-sized balls with dampened hands. Roll in coconut, coating well. Store in an airtight container in the refrigerator.

Serves Forty-Eight
Preparation Time: 15 minutes, plus chilling time

Rum Balls

*These can be stored indefinitely in the refrigerator—
or until your family discovers them.*

Ingredients

2^1/$_2$ cups crushed vanilla wafers
^{1}/$_2$ cup sifted confectioners' sugar
1 cup chopped pecans
6 ounces chocolate chips, melted
^{1}/$_2$ cup light rum
3 tablespoons white corn syrup
1 cup sugar

Directions

Combine the cookie crumbs, confectioners' sugar and pecans in a medium bowl. Add the melted chocolate, rum and corn syrup and mix well. Chill for 1 hour. Shape into 1-inch balls and roll in the sugar. Store in an airtight container in the refrigerator.

Serves Forty-Eight
Preparation Time: 15 minutes, plus chilling time

Fudgy Raspberry Brownies

*If chocolate isn't your favorite flavor, then raspberries are sure to be,
and the combination is almost unbeatable.*

Ingredients

2 egg whites or ^{1}/$_4$ cup egg substitute
^{1}/$_3$ cup low-fat plain yogurt
1 teaspoon vanilla extract
1 (family-size) package fudge brownie mix
3 to 4 tablespoons all-fruit seedless raspberry preserves

Directions

Combine the egg whites, yogurt and vanilla in a large mixer bowl and mix well. Add the brownie mix and mix until smooth; batter will be stiff. Spoon into a 9x13-inch baking dish sprayed with nonstick cooking spray. Bake at 350 degrees for 22 to 24 minutes or until brownies test done; do not overbake. Cool in the pan on a wire rack. Spread with the raspberry preserves. Cut into squares.

Serves Twenty-Four
Preparation Time: 10 minutes, plus cooling time
Cooking Time: 22 to 24 minutes

Glazed Key Lime Cookies

*The juice and grated rind of the Key lime, native to Florida, lends
its flavor to these glazed almond cookies*

Ingredients

2/3 cup almonds
2/3 cup confectioners' sugar, sifted
11 tablespoons unsalted butter, softened
1 egg
2 teaspoons grated Key lime rind
Salt to taste
1 1/2 cups plus 2 tablespoons flour
3 tablespoons confectioners' sugar, sifted
1 egg yolk
1 tablespoon key lime juice

Directions

Process the almonds with 2/3 cup confectioners' sugar in a food processor
or blender for 10 seconds or until finely ground. Combine with the butter in
a mixer bowl and beat until smooth. Beat in 1 egg, lime rind and salt. Add
the flour all at once and mix just until incorporated; do not overmix. Shape
into a ball, wrap in plastic wrap and chill for 3 hours or longer.

Divide the dough into halves, leaving 1 portion in the refrigerator. Roll
1 portion on a generously floured surface. Cut into 2-inch cookies and place
on a cookie sheet. Repeat with the remaining dough. Chill for 30 minutes.
Blend 3 tablespoons confectioners' sugar with the egg yolk and lime juice in
a small bowl. Brush over the cookies.

Bake at 350 degrees for 15 minutes or just until the edges are light
brown. Remove to a wire rack to cool. Store in an airtight container.

Serves Forty-Eight
Preparation Time: 30 minutes, plus chilling time
Cooking Time: 15 minutes

Mocha Chocolate Chip Cookies

Mocha, the combination of chocolate and coffee, is a time-honored favorite and the flavor of coffee gives these chocolate chip cookies a different twist.

Ingredients

3 cups semisweet chocolate chips
4 ounces unsweetened baking chocolate
$1/2$ cup butter
$1/2$ cup flour
$1/2$ teaspoon baking powder
$1/2$ teaspoon salt
4 eggs, at room temperature
$1^1/2$ cups sugar
$1^1/2$ tablespoons instant coffee granules
2 teaspoons vanilla extract

Directions

Melt half the chocolate chips and the unsweetened chocolate with the butter in a double boiler over hot water, stirring to mix well. Mix the flour, baking powder and salt together. Combine the eggs, sugar, coffee granules and vanilla in a large mixer bowl and beat at high speed for 2 minutes. Stir in the chocolate mixture. Add the flour mixture and mix well. Stir in the remaining chocolate chips.

Drop onto cookie sheets lined with baking parchment or waxed paper. Bake at 350 degrees for 8 minutes or until cookies are set but soft inside; outside will appear cracked. Cool completely on the baking sheets.

Serves Eighty
Preparation Time: 20 minutes
Cooking Time: 8 minutes

Frosted Orange Cream Chip Cookies

*These chocolate chip cookies take on a Florida flavor with the
addition of orange juice and grated orange rind.*

For the cookies

2^1/$_2$ cups flour
^{1}/$_2$ teaspoon salt
1 cup shortening
1 cup sugar
4 ounces cream cheese, softened
2 eggs
2 teaspoons orange juice
1 teaspoon grated orange rind
1 cup chocolate chips

For the frosting

4 ounces cream cheese, softened
2 cups sifted confectioners' sugar
1 teaspoon orange juice
1 teaspoon grated orange rind

Garnish

Strips of orange rind or chocolate chips

To prepare the cookies

Sift the flour and salt into a small bowl. Cream the shortening, sugar
and cream cheese in a large mixer bowl until light and fluffy. Beat in the eggs
1 at a time. Add the orange juice, orange rind and flour mixture and mix well.
Stir in the chocolate chips. Drop by rounded teaspoonfuls 2 inches apart onto
lightly greased cookie sheets. Bake at 350 degrees for 12 minutes or until the
edges are light brown. Remove to wire racks to cool.

To prepare the frosting

Beat the cream cheese in a mixer bowl until light. Add the confectioners'
sugar gradually, beating until fluffy. Add the orange juice and orange rind and
mix well. Spread on the cooled cookies. Garnish with strips of orange rind or
chocolate chips.

Serves Seventy-Two
Preparation Time:15 minutes, plus cooling time
Cooking Time: 12 minutes

Spiced Rum Ginger Cookies

Crystallized ginger is ginger that has been preserved by cooking in a sugar syrup and then coated with coarse sugar. It can be found in most supermarkets.

Ingredients

1 cup unsalted butter, softened   1 cup confectioners' sugar
2¹/₂ cups flour   ¹/₂ cup spiced rum
3 tablespoons chopped crystallized ginger
1 teaspoon ground ginger   Salt to taste

Directions

Cream the butter and confectioners' sugar in a mixer bowl until light. Add the remaining ingredients; mix well. Shape into a roll 2¹/₂ inches in diameter and wrap in plastic wrap. Chill in the refrigerator for 2 hours or in the freezer for 45 minutes. Slice ¹/₄ inch thick and place on cookie sheets. Bake at 400 degrees for 10 to 12 minutes or until light brown. Remove to a wire rack to cool.

Serves Seventy-Two
Preparation Time: 15 minutes, plus chilling time
Cooking Time: 10 to 12 minutes

Santa's Whisker Cookies

This cookie dough will keep in the refrigerator for several weeks, so make several batches to have ready for freshly baked cookies for gifts and holiday entertaining.

Ingredients

1 cup butter, softened   1 cup sugar   2 tablespoons milk
1 teaspoon vanilla extract   2¹/₂ cups flour
³/₄ cup finely chopped red and green candied cherries
¹/₂ cup finely chopped pecans   ³/₄ cup flaked coconut

Directions

Cream the butter and sugar in a large mixer bowl until light and fluffy. Blend in the milk and vanilla. Stir in the flour, cherries and pecans. Shape into 2 rolls 8 inches long and 2 inches in diameter. Roll in coconut. Wrap in plastic wrap and chill for several hours to several weeks. Slice ¹/₄ inch thick and place on ungreased cookie sheets. Bake at 375 degrees for 12 minutes or until the edges are golden brown. Remove to a wire rack to cool.

Serves Sixty
Preparation Time: 15 minutes, plus chilling time
Cooking Time: 12 minutes

White Chocolate Almond Balls

These are special cookies and pretty enough to grace the most elegant tea table or dessert buffet.

Ingredients

$1/2$ cup blanched slivered almonds
$3/4$ cup unsalted butter, softened
$1/2$ cup confectioners' sugar
$1/2$ teaspoon salt
2 teaspoons almond extract
2 cups flour
10 ounces white chocolate
$2^1/3$ cups flaked coconut

Directions

Spread the almonds on a baking sheet. Toast at 325 degrees for 8 to 10 minutes or until golden brown. Cool and chop. Beat the butter, confectioners' sugar, salt and almond extract in a mixer bowl until light and fluffy. Beat in the flour at low speed just until incorporated. Add the almonds and mix. Chill until firm. Shape into 1-inch balls and place on an ungreased baking sheet.

Bake at 325 degrees for 15 to 18 minutes or until golden brown on the bottom. Remove to a wire rack to cool. Reduce the oven temperature to 250 degrees.

Chop the white chocolate into a small ovenproof bowl. Place in 250-degree oven until melted. Drop the cookies 1 at a time into the chocolate, coating well. Remove with 2 forks, allowing excess chocolate to drip back into bowl. Drop into coconut and press lightly to coat well. Place on a rack to dry.

Serves Forty
Preparation Time: 30 minutes, plus chilling time
Cooking Time: 25 minutes

Paper Bag Apple Pie

This is a time-honored recipe using a brown paper bag, from the days when all bags were made of new material. Now you must take care to select a paper bag made of nonrecycled material, as heating recycled bags releases toxic chemicals.

For the pastry

1¹/2 cups flour
1¹/2 teaspoons sugar
¹/2 cup vegetable oil
2 tablespoons cold milk
1 teaspoon salt

For the filling

4 cups sliced peeled Granny Smith or sour apples
2 tablespoons flour
1¹/2 cups sugar
1 teaspoon cinnamon

For the topping

¹/2 cup flour
¹/2 cup sugar
¹/2 cup margarine or butter

To prepare the pastry

Mix the flour, sugar, oil, milk and salt in a bowl and mix to form dough. Roll on a floured surface and fit into a pie plate. Trim and crimp the edge.

To prepare the filling

Toss the apples with the flour, sugar and cinnamon in a bowl. Spoon into the pastry.

To prepare the topping and bake the pie

Mix the flour, sugar and margarine in a bowl until crumbly. Sprinkle over the pie. Place in a brown paper bag and close the opening. Cut 4 or 5 slits in the bag and place on a baking sheet. Bake at 350 degrees for 1¹/2 hours.

Serves Eight
Preparation Time: 30 minutes
Cooking Time: 1¹/2 hours

Coconut Cream Pie

This is an old-fashioned pie like your grandmother used to make and sure to be on everyone's list of comfort foods and holiday favorites.

Ingredients

1 unbaked (9-inch) pie shell
3/4 cup sugar
1/3 cup flour or 3 tablespoons cornstarch
1/4 teaspoon salt
2 cups milk
3 egg yolks, slightly beaten
2 tablespoons butter
1 teaspoon vanilla extract
1 cup coconut
3 egg whites, at room temperature
1/4 teaspoon cream of tartar
1/2 teaspoon vanilla extract
6 tablespoons sugar
1/3 cup coconut

Directions

Prick the bottom and side of the pie shell. Bake at 450 degrees for 10 to 12 minutes or until golden brown. Combine 3/4 cup sugar, flour and salt in a large microwave-safe bowl. Stir in the milk gradually. Microwave on High for 8 to 10 minutes or until bubbly, stirring occasionally. Microwave for 2 minutes longer, stirring every 30 seconds. Stir a small amount of the hot mixture into the egg yolks; stir the egg yolks into the hot mixture. Microwave for 2 minutes longer, stirring every 30 seconds. Stir in the butter, 1 teaspoon vanilla and 1 cup coconut. Spoon into the cooled pie shell.

Beat the egg whites with the cream of tartar and 1/2 teaspoon vanilla until soft peaks form. Add 6 tablespoons sugar gradually, beating constantly until stiff peaks form. Spread over the warm filling, making high peaks with the back of a spoon and sealing to the edge of the pie shell. Sprinkle with 1/3 cup coconut. Bake at 350 degrees for 12 to 15 minutes or until the meringue is golden brown. Serve warm or at room temperature.

Serves Nine
Preparation Time: 15 minutes
Cooking Time: 30 minutes

Classic Key Lime Pie

The Key lime, named for the Florida Keys, is native to the area. It is generally smaller, rounder and more yellow in color than the Persian lime, which is more widely available. A true Key lime pie is yellow rather than the green we sometimes associate with lime.

Ingredients

1 unbaked (9-inch) pie shell
4 egg yolks
1 (14-ounce) can sweetened condensed milk
1/3 cup Key lime juice
1/3 cup sifted confectioners' sugar
4 egg whites, at room temperature
1/2 teaspoon cream of tartar
6 tablespoons sugar

Directions

Prick the bottom and side of the pie shell with a fork. Bake at 450 degrees for 10 to 12 minutes or until golden brown. Cool to room temperature. Beat the egg yolks at medium speed until thick and lemon-colored. Add the condensed milk, Key lime juice and confectioners' sugar, mixing well. Spoon into the pie shell. Beat the egg whites with the cream of tartar at high speed for 1 minute. Add the sugar 1 tablespoon at a time, beating for 2 to 4 minutes or until stiff peaks form. Spread over the filling, sealing to the edge of the pie shell. Bake at 350 degrees for 12 to 15 minutes or until the meringue is golden brown.

Variation: Instead of the meringue, top the pie with a sauce of raspberries and Grand Marnier. Drain two 10-ounce packages of frozen raspberries and press through a sieve to remove the seeds. Chill in the refrigerator and add 2 to 3 tablespoons Grand Marnier just before serving. Rinse 2 pints of fresh raspberries and sprinkle with 1/4 cup confectioners' sugar. Spread with the raspberry purée and top with the fresh raspberries, or nap the plates with the purée and top the servings with the fresh raspberries.

Serves Eight
Preparation Time: 15 minutes, plus cooling time
Cooking Time: 30 minutes

Low-Fat Key Lime Pie

You can have your diet and eat pie, too, with this low-fat version of the traditional Key lime pie. It is especially good to top off light summer meals.

Ingredients

1 teaspoon unflavored gelatin
$1/4$ cup water
$1/2$ cup Key lime juice
Grated zest of 2 Key limes
$3/4$ cup sugar
1 cup low-fat cottage cheese
1 cup low-fat plain yogurt
1 graham cracker pie shell

Directions

Soften the gelatin in the water in a saucepan. Heat over low heat until the gelatin dissolves, stirring constantly. Add the lime juice, lime zest and sugar. Cook until the sugar dissolves and the mixture begins to thicken, stirring constantly. Spoon into a large bowl and whisk until lukewarm.

Process the cottage cheese and yogurt in a blender until smooth; do not use a food processor. Fold into the lime mixture. Spoon into the pie shell. Chill for 4 hours or until set. Serve chilled.

Serves Eight
Preparation Time: 20 minutes, plus chilling time

Plum Tart

Surprise your friends and family with the easy dessert that is a little different and uses a popular fruit for which we have fewer recipes.

Ingredients

1/2 cup unsalted butter, softened
1 cup sugar
1 cup unbleached flour
1 teaspoon baking powder
2 eggs
Salt to taste
12 purple plums, cut into halves
1/4 to 1/2 cup confectioners' sugar
1 to 2 tablespoons lemon juice
1 teaspoon cinnamon

Directions

Cream the butter and sugar in a mixer bowl until light and fluffy. Add the flour, baking powder, eggs and salt and beat until smooth. Spoon into a 9-inch springform pan.

Arrange the plums cut side down on the top. Sprinkle with the confectioners' sugar, lemon juice and cinnamon. Bake at 350 degrees for 1 hour. Serve warm or at room temperature with ice cream.

Serves Eight
Preparation Time: 15 minutes
Cooking Time: 1 hour

Strawberry and Kiwifruit Tart

The contrasting colors and flavors of the strawberries and the kiwifruit make this tart a beautiful addition to the table as well as the menu.

For the pastry

1/2 cup butter, softened
1/2 cup sugar
1 egg yolk
1 teaspoon vanilla extract
1/2 teaspoon almond extract
1 1/2 cups flour
1/2 cup sliced almonds, toasted

For the filling and glaze

8 ounces cream cheese, softened
2 tablespoons sugar
2 tablespoons amaretto or 1/2 teaspoon almond extract
1 teaspoon vanilla extract
3 to 4 fresh kiwifruit, thinly sliced
1 pint fresh strawberries
1/4 cup apricot jam
1 tablespoon water
1/4 cup sliced almonds, toasted

To prepare the pastry

Cream the butter and sugar in a mixer bowl until light and fluffy. Beat in the egg yolk and flavorings. Add the flour and almonds and mix to form dough. Press into an 11-inch tart pan with a removable bottom. Prick with a fork. Bake at 375 degrees for 10 minutes or until golden brown. Cool on a wire rack.

To prepare the filling and glaze the tart

Beat the cream cheese and sugar in a mixer bowl until smooth. Add the amaretto and vanilla. Spread in the cooled tart shell. Chill until firm. Arrange the slices of kiwifruit around the outer edge, overlapping the slices by 1/4 to 1/2 inch. Reserve several of the whole strawberries and slice the remaining strawberries. Arrange the strawberry slices in a circle inside the kiwifruit. Fill the center with the remaining strawberry slices and the reserved whole strawberries. Whisk the jam with the water in a saucepan. Cook for 30 seconds or until the jam melts, whisking constantly. Cool slightly. Brush over the fruit. Sprinkle with the almonds.

Serves Twelve
Preparation Time: 20 minutes, plus cooling and chilling time
Cooking Time: 10 minutes

A Taste of
the Town

Taste of the Town

Photograph Recipes

Broiled Pompano with White Wine Sauce

For the sauce

1 bunch green onions with tops, chopped
1 cup butter
$^1/_3$ cup flour
2 cups heavy cream
$^1/_4$ clove of garlic, chopped
1 ounce fresh lemon juice
Salt and pepper to taste
6 ounces Chablis

For the fish

4 (5-ounce) pompano fillets
1 tablespoon butter
Salt and pepper to taste

To prepare the sauce

Sauté the green onions in the butter in a sauté pan for 10 minutes or until tender but not brown. Stir in the flour. Cook for 10 minutes, stirring constantly; do not brown. Stir in the cream, garlic, lemon juice, salt and pepper. Cook until thickened, stirring constantly. Simmer over low heat for 30 minutes. Add the wine and remove from the heat; keep warm.

To prepare the fish

Place the fish fillets in a broiler pan. Top with the butter, salt and pepper. Broil for 5 to 8 minutes or until the fish is cooked through and flakes easily; do not overcook. Serve with the warm sauce.

Serves Four
Preparation Time: 10 minutes
Cooking Time: 1 hour

Red Velvet Cake

For the cake

3³/₄ cups self-rising flour
2¹/₄ cups sugar
1¹/₂ teaspoons baking cocoa   1¹/₂ teaspoons baking soda
3 eggs   1¹/₂ teaspoons vinegar
2¹/₄ cups vegetable oil
1¹/₂ cups buttermilk
1¹/₂ teaspoons vanilla extract
3 ounces red food coloring

For the frosting

16 ounces cream cheese, softened
1¹/₂ cups butter, softened
2 (16-ounce) packages confectioners' sugar
3 cups chopped pecans
Whole pecans

To prepare the cake

Mix the flour, sugar, baking cocoa and baking soda in a bowl. Add the eggs, vinegar, oil, buttermilk, vanilla and food coloring and mix well. Spoon into 3 greased and floured 9-inch cake pans. Bake at 350 degrees for 45 to 60 minutes or until the layers pull from the sides of the pans. Cool in the pans for 10 minutes; remove to a wire rack to cool completely.

To prepare the frosting and frost the cake

Beat the cream cheese and butter in a mixer bowl until light. Beat in the confectioners' sugar and chopped pecans. Spread between the layers and over the top and side of the cake. Top with a circle of whole pecans.

Serves Sixteen
Preparation Time: 30 minutes
Cooking Time: 45 to 60 minutes

The Bubble Room Restaurants

Chocolate Bread Pudding with Amaretto Fudge Sauce

For the pudding

8 cups bread, cake or muffin scraps
1 quart milk   2 cups half-and-half
10 eggs
2$^{1}/_{2}$ cups sugar $^{1}/_{2}$ cup nuts
1 cup chocolate chips
1 cup dried cherries or currants, soaked in
Grand Marnier or any liqueur
1$^{1}/_{2}$ to 2 cups fudge sauce
Whipped cream

For the fudge sauce

2 cups heavy cream
16 ounces chocolate chips
Amaretto to taste

To prepare the pudding

Combine the bread scraps with the milk and half-and-half in a bowl and mix well. Beat in the eggs and sugar. Stir in the nuts, chocolate chips and dried cherries. Spoon into a buttered and sugared large square baking pan. Cover with buttered foil and place in a larger pan of water. Bake at 325 degrees for 1 hour or until set. Remove the foil cover. Bake for 20 minutes longer. Cool to room temperature. Serve with the fudge sauce and top with whipped cream.

To prepare the fudge sauce

Bring the heavy cream to a boil in a saucepan. Stir in the chocolate chips until melted. Add the Amaretto.

Serves Sixteen
Preparation Time: 20 minutes
Cooking Time: 1$^{1}/_{2}$ hours

Morning, Noon 'n' Night

Chicken Capellini Pignoli

Ingredients

6 ounces boneless skinless chicken breasts, julienned
2 ounces virgin olive oil
1 tablespoon chopped garlic
10 ounces capellini, cooked
3 ounces sun-dried tomatoes, julienned
3 ounces red bell pepper, chopped
4 or 5 large broccoli florets
2 ounces pignoli, oven-roasted
4 ounces red wine vinegar Italian salad dressing
Salt to taste

Garnish

Parsley

Directions

Rinse the chicken and pat dry. Sauté in the olive oil in a heated sauté pan for 2 minutes, tossing frequently. Add the garlic. Sauté for 10 seconds. Add the pasta, sun-dried tomatoes, bell pepper, broccoli, pignoli and salad dressing; toss to mix well. Season to taste. Spoon into a large pasta bowl. Garnish with parsley.

Serves Four
Preparation Time: 10 minutes
Cooking Time: 10 minutes

Mud Pie

Ingredients

8 ounces chocolate wafers, crushed
$1/4$ cup melted butter
1 gallon coffee ice cream, softened
$1^1/2$ cups fudge sauce, chilled

Garnish

Whipped cream
Almonds

Directions

Mix the cookie crumbs and butter in a bowl. Press into a 9-inch pie plate. Spread with the ice cream and top with the fudge sauce. Freeze for 10 hours. Serve on chilled dessert plates. Garnish the servings with whipped cream and almonds.

Serves Eight
Preparation Time: 15 minutes, plus freezing time

THE CHART HOUSE
Steak - Seafood - Prime Rib

Bread Pudding

Ingredients

3 cups sugar
9 eggs
$^1/_2$ gallon milk
1 cup butter, softened
2 teaspoons vanilla extract
2 loaves white bread, cut into $^1/_2$-inch cubes
1 teaspoon cinnamon
2 teaspoons sugar

Directions

Combine 3 cups sugar, eggs, milk, butter and vanilla in a large bowl and mix well. Fold in the bread cubes. Spoon into a large baking pan. Sprinkle with a mixture of the cinnamon and 2 teaspoons sugar. Place in a larger pan filled halfway with water. Bake at 350 degrees for $2^1/_2$ to 3 hours.

Serves Twenty-Four
Preparation Time: 15 minutes
Cooking Time: $2^1/_2$ to 3 hours

Clancey's
Informal Dining

Coco Loco Mousse with Spiced Rum Sauce

For the chocolate shells

2 pounds coating chocolate
1/2 cup (or to taste) chopped macadamia nuts, toasted

For the mousse and rum sauce

8 egg yolks   1 1/2 cups sugar
5 tablespoons cornstarch
6 1/2 cups milk   1 vanilla bean, split
1 1/2 ounces (12 sheets or 5 tablespoons) plumed gelatine
1 small can coconut cream
1 cup shredded coconut   2 cups whipped cream
Rum to taste

To prepare the chocolate shells

Melt the chocolate in a heavy saucepan over low heat. Stir in the nuts. Dip a blown-up balloon halfway into the chocolate. Let stand until firm. Dip again. Chill until firm. Pop balloon carefully and remove.

To prepare the mousse

Beat the egg yolks and sugar in a mixer bowl until thick and lemon-colored. Beat in the cornstarch. Bring the milk and the vanilla bean to a boil in a saucepan. Stir a small amount of the hot milk into the egg mixture; stir the egg mixture into the hot milk. Cook until thickened, stirring constantly. Strain into a bowl and cool in an ice bath.

Combine 4 cups of the custard with the melted gelatine in a bowl. Cool over an ice bath until slightly thickened. Fold in the coconut cream, coconut and whipped cream. Spoon into the chocolate shells. Chill until firm. Mix the remaining custard with rum. Serve over the mousse.

Serves Six
Preparation Time: 1 hour, plus chilling time
Cooking Time: 15 minutes

KING'S CROWN

Shrimp Provençal

Ingredients

1 leek, chopped
1 stalk celery, thinly sliced
2 tablespoons olive oil
1 cup dry white wine
1 tablespoon tomato paste
1 pound shrimp, peeled, deveined
12 oil-cured olives
$^1/_2$ cup sun-dried tomatoes
2 cloves of garlic, minced
1 teaspoon thyme
1 teaspoon rosemary
Salt and pepper to taste

Directions

Sauté the leek and celery in the heated olive oil in a large skillet over low heat for 5 minutes. Stir in the wine and tomato paste and bring to a boil. Add the shrimp, olives, sun-dried tomatoes, garlic, thyme, rosemary, salt and pepper. Cook just until the shrimp are cooked through.

Serves Four
Preparation Time: 10 minutes
Cooking Time: 15 minutes

Grouper Maison

Ingredients

4 (6-ounce) grouper fillets
3 bananas, cut into quarters lengthwise
4 ounces light brown sugar
1/4 cup bread crumbs
2 cups pineapple juice
12 ounces béarnaise sauce
4 ounces sliced almonds, sautéed

Directions

Arrange the grouper fillets in a 9x9-inch baking dish. Top with the banana pieces, brown sugar and bread crumbs. Add the pineapple juice. Bake at 375 degrees for 10 minutes or until the fish is cooked through. Serve with béarnaise sauce and sautéed almonds. For a special presentation, arrange 2 or 3 leaves from the top of a pineapple on the serving plate at 1 end of the fillet to resemble a pineapple.

Serves Four
Preparation Time: 15 minutes
Cooking Time: 10 minutes

A Tradition of
Waterfront Dining

Charcoal-Grilled Grouper with Mango Butter

For the mango butter

1$^{1}/_{5}$ cups white wine
1 bunch fresh mint, chopped
1 small mango, puréed   1 banana, puréed
Juice and grated zest of 1 orange
Cinnamon to taste   3 egg yolks
1 pound butter, softened

For the fish

4 to 6 (8-ounce) grouper fillets
$^{1}/_{4}$ cup melted butter
Seasoned salt to taste

To prepare the mango butter

Combine the wine and mint in a saucepan. Cook until reduced to $^{1}/_{3}$ cup. Cool to room temperature. Combine the mango, banana, orange juice and orange zest in a bowl. Add the wine mixture and mix well. Mix in the cinnamon and egg yolks. Cream the butter in a mixer bowl until light. Add to the fruit mixture and mix well.

To prepare the fish

Brush the fish with the melted butter and sprinkle with the seasoned salt. Grill until cooked through. Serve with the mango butter.

Serves Four to Six
Preparation Time: 15 minutes, plus cooling time
Cooking Time: 20 minutes

Lobster Bisque

Ingredients

1 carrot, chopped
1 onion, chopped
1 stalk celery, chopped
1 tablespoon melted unsalted butter
1 tablespoon tomato paste
5 ounces cognac
Meat of 1 Maine lobster, chopped
8 ounces white wine
16 ounces whipping cream
Salt and pepper to taste

Directions

Sauté the carrot, onion and celery in the melted butter in a 32-ounce saucepan until tender but not brown. Add the tomato paste and cognac. Cook until reduced to desired consistency. Add the lobster. Cook for 2 minutes, stirring constantly. Stir in the white wine, cream, salt and pepper. Simmer for 1 hour. Strain liquid to serve.

Serves Four
Preparation Time: 10 minutes
Cooking Time: 1¹/₄ hours

Peter's
La Cuisine

Grouper Fresca

Ingredients

4 medium vine-ripened tomatoes, chopped
3 ounces fennel, chopped
2 tablespoons chopped rosemary
2 tablespoons chopped basil
2 tablespoons chopped thyme
3 tablespoons chopped parsley
2 ounces olive oil
Salt and pepper to taste
8 grouper fillets

Directions

Combine the tomatoes, fennel, rosemary, basil, thyme, parsley, olive oil, salt and pepper in a bowl and mix well. Let stand at room temperature for 1 hour to blend flavors.

Grill the grouper until it flakes easily. Serve with the tomato fresca.

Serves Eight
Preparation Time: 10 minutes, plus standing time
Cooking Time: 15 minutes

Pepper Salad Dressing

Ingredients

5 cups mayonnaise, chilled
2 cups evaporated milk
2 cups finely chopped Greek peperoncini peppers
2 cups peperoncini juice
1 cup 1-inch green onion pieces
3 ounces lemon juice
1 ounce Tabasco sauce
$^1/_2$ ounce salt
1 ounce white pepper

Directions

Combine the chilled mayonnaise, evaporated milk, peperoncini, peperoncini juice, green onions, lemon juice, Tabasco sauce, salt and white pepper in a bowl and mix well. Chill in an airtight container in the refrigerator for 1 to 7 days.

Yields Twelve Cups
Preparation Time: 15 minutes

Bourbon Street Fillet

Ingredients

2 (3-ounce) tenderloin medallions
¹/₄ cup fresh mushroom quarters
¹/₄ teaspoon minced garlic
¹/₄ teaspoon minced shallots
¹/₄ cup chopped green onions
Rosemary, thyme and cracked black pepper to taste
Butter and/or oil for sautéing
³/₄ ounce sour mash bourbon
1 tablespoon butter

Directions

Sauté the medallions, mushrooms, garlic, shallots, green onions, rosemary, thyme and pepper in a small amount of butter and oil in a sauté pan for 8 minute for medium-rare. Add the bourbon and ignite; allow the flames to die down. Whisk in 1 tablespoon butter over low heat; do not boil. Serve the medallions with the sauce.

Serves One
Preparation Time: 15 minutes
Cooking Time: 8 to 10 minutes

Etcetera

Nutritional Profile Guidelines

The editors have attempted to present these recipes in a form that allows approximate nutritional values to be computed. Persons with dietary or health problems or whose diets require close monitor should not rely solely on the nutritional information provided. They should consult their physicians a registered dietitian for specific information.

Abbreviations for Nutritional Profile

Cal — Calories
Prot — Protein
Carbo — Carbohydrates
Fiber — Dietary Fiber
T Fat — Total Fat

Chol — Cholesterol
Sod — Sodium
g — grams
mg — milligrams

Nutritional information for these recipes is computed from information derived from many sourc including materials supplied by the United States Department of Agriculture, computer data bank and journals in which the information is assumed to be in the public domain. However, many specialty items, new products, and processed foods may not be available from these sources or may vary from the average values used in these profiles. More information on new and/or specific prod may be obtained by reading the nutrient labels. Unless otherwise specified, the nutritional profile these recipes is based on all measurements being level.

If a choice of ingredients has been given, the nutritional profile reflects the first option. If a choice of amounts has been given, the nutritional profile reflects the greater amount.

Alcoholic ingredients have been analyzed for the basic ingredients. Cooking causes the evaporation of alcohol, thus decreasing caloric content.

Buttermilk, sour cream, and **yogurt** are the types available commercially.

Cake Mixes which are prepared using package directions include 3 eggs and ½ cup oil.

Chicken, cooked for boning and chopping, has been roasted; this method yields the lowest caloric values.

Cottage cheese is cream-style with 4.2% creaming mixture. Dry curd cottage cheese has no creaming mixture.

Eggs are all large. To avoid raw eggs that may carry salmonella, as in eggnog or 6–week muffin batter, use an equivalent amount of commercial egg substitute.

Flour is unsifted all-purpose flour.

Garnishes, serving suggestions, and other optional additions and variations are not included in the profile.

Margarine and **butter** are regular, not whipped or presoftened.

Milk is whole milk, 3.5% butterfat. Lowfat milk is 1% butterfat. Evaporated milk is whole milk with 60% of the water removed.

Oil is any type of vegetable cooking oil.

Shortening is hydrogenated vegetable shortening.

Salt and other ingredients to taste as noted in the ingredients have not been included in the nutritional profile.

Photograph Recipes
Grilled Swordfish with Salsa Fresca on page 173
Herbed Biscuits on page 53
Classic Key Lime Pie on page 217

Pg #	Recipe Title (Approx Per Serving)	Cal	Prot (g)	Carbo (g)	T Fat (g)	% Cal from Fat	Chol (mg)	Fiber (g)	Sod (mg)
11	Grilled Antipasto Platter	247	8	12	20	69	22	4	871
12	Beef Wellington Miniatures	117	6	6	7	56	19	<1	251
13	Bleu Cheese and Pear Pizza	361	14	39	17	42	45	4	343
14	Polenta Toast with Roasted Peppers	69	3	9	2	30	1	1	325
15	Marinated Mushrooms	158	1	5	14	75	0	1	272
16	Crab-Stuffed Mushrooms	79	5	3	6	65	16	1	114
17	Baked Stuffed Mussels	478	53	21	19	36	146	1	939
17	Lime-Glazed Seafood Kabobs	136	12	1	9	61	52	<1	175
18	Oysters with Bacon and Balsamic Vinegar	220	6	3	21	83	71	<1	381
19	Marinated Shrimp	113	10	2	7	58	89	<1	374
20	Shark Seviche	254	14	11	18	62	31	2	53
20	Spinach and Basil Hors d'Oeuvre	30	2	5	<1	11	<1	<1	78
21	Baby Brie in Phyllo	217	8	12	16	64	47	<1	338
21	Baked Brie with Pecans	347	13	14	26	65	57	1	360
22	Chick-Pea and Pesto Spread	136	6	9	9	58	13	<1	258
22	Garbanzo Paté	45	2	6	2	29	0	1	27
23	Lobster Spread	97	6	1	8	72	34	<1	170
23	Mullet Spread	67	4	1	5	69	25	<1	143
24	Mushroom Spread	169	5	6	15	76	40	1	267
25	Alligator Eye	42	1	3	4	69	0	1	228
25	Aloha Shrimp Dip	145	6	12	8	50	56	1	129
26	Tangy Tortilla Dip	21	2	4	<1	1	0	<1	41
26	Bleu Cheese Fondue	158	6	2	15	81	44	0	292
29	Gratin of Fresh Fruit	166	3	24	7	36	169	3	11
30	Tropical Fruit Crisp	128	1	33	<1	2	0	2	2
31	Fruit Puff	179	6	34	2	11	71	3	60
32	Fresh Fruit Omelet	327	11	50	10	27	151	3	231
33	Cheesy Egg and Mushroom Casserole	296	14	13	21	64	297	1	455
34	Lobster and Fresh Vegetable Frittata	408	26	8	31	67	263	2	399
35	Vegetable Frittata	385	28	11	26	60	356	3	272
36	Herbed Eggs in Toast Baskets	184	12	17	8	38	266	2	1187
37	Orange Oatmeal Pie	479	15	42	28	53	249	2	365
38	Veal and Spinach Pie	449	26	26	27	54	113	2	497
39	Individual Seafood Quiches	267	8	14	20	68	69	1	301
40	Fiesta Quiche	162	11	19	5	26	6	2	602
41	Fresh Tomato Tart	241	8	20	15	54	26	1	442
42	Tomato Quiche	434	10	23	34	70	179	2	573
43	Fresh Tomato Purée	233	5	29	13	46	31	8	699

Pg #	Recipe Title (Approx Per Serving)	Cal	Prot (g)	Carbo (g)	T Fat (g)	% Cal from Fat	Chol (mg)	Fiber (g)	Sod (mg)
44	Cheese Linzer Torte	425	13	24	32	66	132	1	611
45	Classic Cuban Sandwich	777	45	67	36	42	115	4	1771
46	Baked Swiss Grits	326	12	22	21	59	65	2	579
47	Pine Island Popovers	118	5	14	5	37	84	<1	239
48	Orange Muffins	393	5	51	20	45	78	1	263
49	Sunshine Muffins	303	5	48	11	32	37	2	263
50	Carrot Bread	218	3	30	10	41	35	1	154
51	Miniature Raspberry Loaves	276	8	49	6	19	20	3	319
52	Avocado Toast	182	5	16	12	56	5	3	271
52	Bleu Bread	285	6	21	20	63	7	1	594
53	Herbed Biscuits	123	2	12	9	58	13	<1	355
53	Savory Bread	152	6	21	6	32	10	1	551
54	Chocolate Biscotti	126	3	20	6	36	13	1	34
55	Almond Iced Tea	157	<1	39	<1	<1	0	<1	3
55	Morning Coffee Cooler	82	8	12	<1	4	3	0	115
56	Coffee Punch	250	3	16	20	71	70	1	60
56	Berry Pineapple Shake	125	2	31	1	7	0	6	7
57	Fresh Citrus Cooler	495	2	126	<1	1	0	1	10
57	Kiwifruit Float	231	3	39	8	31	29	1	63
58	Minty Lemon-Lime Freeze	124	5	26	1	4	2	1	64
58	Southwest Florida Sunrise Shake	175	2	43	1	6	0	6	3
59	Bloody Mary Mix	42	2	11	<1	3	0	2	1240
59	Peach Fuzzies	237	<1	32	<1	1	0	1	6
60	Sangria Blanca	196	1	23	<1	2	0	3	7
60	Turquoise Margaritas	176	<1	21	<1	<1	0	<1	21
63	Asparagus Soup	217	8	13	14	54	38	3	560
64	Collard Green and Bean Soup	459	42	41	15	28	71	13	1475
65	Curried Cauliflower and Potato Soup	138	8	21	3	20	9	3	348
66	Gazpacho	92	2	11	6	50	0	3	170
67	White Gazpacho	212	7	14	15	62	48	1	1020
68	Golden Pepper and Tomato Soup	110	2	11	8	59	27	2	18
69	Cream of Peanut Soup	229	12	15	14	54	37	1	898
70	Roquefort and Spinach Soup	341	9	6	30	78	89	2	808
71	Cold Squash Soup	267	4	12	23	73	77	3	129
72	Wild Rice Soup	206	7	20	10	41	25	2	691
73	Cioppino	513	40	15	30	52	117	4	934
74	Seafood Black Bean Gumbo[1]	253	34	14	7	24	186	3	741
75	Shrimp and Andouille Sausage Gumbo	486	32	24	30	54	240	4	1983

Pg #	Recipe Title (Approx Per Serving)	Cal	Prot (g)	Carbo (g)	Fat (g)	% Cal from Fat	Chol (mg)	Fiber (g)	Sod (mg)
76	Avocado and Raspberry Salad	201	2	17	16	64	0	4	10
76	Frosty Summer Fruit Salad	260	1	66	<1	2	0	2	2
77	Honeydew Gin Salad	132	2	31	<1	2	0	3	33
78	Melon and Mango Salad	231	3	37	10	36	0	4	32
79	Beef Salad	339	23	30	14	38	45	2	3149
80	Dijon Asparagus and Chicken Pasta Salad	486	23	26	33	60	70	2	743
81	Chinese Chicken Salad	219	16	23	8	31	37	2	934
82	Curried Chicken Salad	464	38	17	28	54	114	3	333
83	Grilled Chicken Salad with Citrus Salsa	410	31	20	21	45	73	5	120
84	Crab Meat and Mango Salad	478	18	28	35	63	76	6	235
85	Lobster Coleslaw with Fresh Herbs	356	30	8	23	59	114	1	736
86	Shrimp and Endive Salad/Dressing	360	6	9	35	84	28	2	105
87	Roasted Pepper and Pasta Salad	387	9	47	18	43	0	3	107
88	Asparagus Salad	115	3	7	9	67	0	3	3
89	Romaine and Orange Salad	173	4	22	9	45	6	1	434
90	Black-Eyed Pea Salad	549	14	43	38	60	0	14	745
91	Broiled Pepper Salad	98	2	11	6	53	0	2	6
92	Chick-Pea and Parsley Salad	228	6	19	15	58	0	6	282
93	Fresh Tomatoes/Buttermilk Dressing	87	2	10	5	49	6	2	349
94	Marinated Tomatoes	128	1	5	12	82	0	1	186
94	Yogurt Tahini Dressing	33	2	2	2	54	5	<1	108
97	Black Bean and Corn Salsa	197	11	39	1	5	0	8	957
98	Green Bean Bundles	168	5	15	11	55	26	5	190
99	Green Beans Caesar	150	6	9	11	62	17	4	201
100	Calico Beans	181	9	37	1	5	2	8	609
101	Broccoli in Orange-Shallot Butter	252	4	10	23	79	62	3	35
102	Broccoli Sauté	81	3	18	1	7	0	3	46
103	Sautéed Brussels Sprout Leaves	121	3	6	10	72	8	3	12
103	Gingered Carrots	75	1	8	5	55	10	2	65
104	Mustard-Glazed Carrots	142	2	16	8	51	21	5	263
104	Sweet Carrot Soufflé	214	5	23	12	48	132	1	138
105	Chayote in Parsley Butter	50	1	6	3	52	8	1	34
106	Leeks au Gratin	197	6	25	9	38	25	4	172
107	Baked Leeks	332	11	45	14	35	42	6	198
108	Mushrooms Provençale	92	3	6	7	66	16	2	64
109	Red Wine Mushrooms	46	2	4	1	25	3	1	250
110	Mushrooms and Peppers	194	2	17	12	55	31	1	267
111	Vidalia Onion Casserole	275	9	25	16	52	47	2	63

Pg #	Recipe Title (Approx Per Serving)	Cal	Prot (g)	Carbo (g)	T Fat (g)	% Cal from Fat	Chol (mg)	Fiber (g)	Sod (mg)
112	Herbed Potato Wheel	211	2	18	15	64	41	1	161
113	Roasted Garlic Mashed Potatoes	388	6	54	17	39	27	4	27
114	Rosemary Potatoes with Garlic	329	5	46	15	39	0	4	524
115	Sautéed Potatoes and Leeks	403	8	81	6	14	16	8	95
115	Snow Peas and Carrots	127	4	19	4	28	10	4	65
116	Spaghetti Squash Casserole	87	6	9	4	34	10	3	181
117	Sweet Potato Chips	448	7	24	36	72	62	4	365
118	Orange-Baked Sweet Potatoes	189	2	30	3	14	8	4	115
119	Caribbean Vegetable Medley	43	1	6	1	27	0	2	50
120	Grilled Vegetables	183	6	20	11	48	11	8	62
121	Vegetable Enchiladas	493	19	67	19	33	30	12	1027
122	Fettucini e Limone	525	14	59	26	45	82	2	254
123	Vermicelli with Mascarpone and Spinach	493	14	60	22	41	70	3	184
124	Cilantro Pesto	325	5	7	31	85	7	3	206
124	Pasta with Pecan-Tomato Sauce	706	14	73	42	52	62	5	250
125	Tortellini Pesto	1134	37	62	85	66	83	4	902
126	Sun-Dried Tomato Sauce for Pasta	207	3	15	15	59	16	4	375
127	Brown and Wild Rice with Almonds	1411	8	512	12	5	0	3	236
128	Fruited Rice Pilaf	230	4	38	8	30	10	3	560
129	Harvest Rice	237	3	50	3	12	0	3	34
130	Nutty Wild Rice	316	8	37	17	46	0	2	636
131	Baked Bananas	409	3	54	23	47	41	4	11
132	Pineapple Bake	677	10	97	29	38	275	2	478
135	Beef on the Rocks	242	39	2	8	30	92	<1	6478
136	Beef Rouladen	219	20	19	6	22	25	4	1391
137	Grilled Beef Kabobs	666	45	36	38	51	108	3	4843
138	Grilled Flank Steak	321	25	8	20	56	76	<1	988
138	London Broil with Mushroom Sauce	482	39	8	33	61	92	2	1492
139	Bleu Cheese Pork Loin	301	39	1	15	45	105	<1	367
139	Herb-Marinated Pork Tenderloin	169	22	11	4	20	56	<1	2097
140	Pork Loin with Apricots	212	29	6	7	30	73	1	134
141	Pork Medallions in Mustard Sauce	620	33	4	52	74	226	1	792
142	Pork Medallions with Sautéed Apples	382	24	31	18	43	143	2	524
143	Grilled Garlic Pork Chops	216	12	4	17	71	35	1	562
144	Grilled Marinated Sweet and Sour Pork	167	21	13	4	19	56	<1	1081
145	Breaded Veal with Lemon and Capers	854	32	43	62	65	285	2	495
146	Veal Chops Italiano	374	37	3	23	57	136	1	239
147	Veal Scalopine	439	28	25	25	52	96	2	145

Pg #	Recipe Title (Approx Per Serving)	Cal	Prot (g)	Carbo (g)	T Fat (g)	% Cal from Fat	Chol (mg)	Fiber (g)	Sod (mg)
148	Brown Bag Chicken	323	49	0	13	37	151	0	1211
149	Parmesan Baked Chicken	382	52	<1	18	44	156	0	262
150	Chicken and Asparagus Pinwheels	286	30	16	10	31	81	2	163
151	Cajun Chicken and Mushrooms	350	33	19	16	41	101	1	432
152	Citrus Chicken Stir-Fry	324	29	19	15	41	72	3	225
153	Gorgonzola Chicken	568	49	10	34	55	140	1	1590
154	Jamaican Chicken	407	55	9	13	28	158	<1	906
155	Spicy Kung Pao Chicken	785	43	74	35	40	72	5	314
156	Lime and Cilantro Chicken/Tomato Salsa	255	29	11	11	39	73	4	79
157	Normandy Chicken	312	30	10	16	47	97	1	886
158	Orange-Glazed Chicken	313	28	14	15	43	73	<1	187
159	Chicken in Pastry Shells	501	23	23	35	63	72	1	863
160	Spinach-Stuffed Chicken in Apricot Sauce	269	33	20	7	22	73	3	300
161	Chicken with Sun-Dried Tomato Sauce	143	16	6	6	40	41	1	216
162	Versatile Baked Chicken	347	28	7	23	60	120	<1	570
163	Turkey Enchiladas	517	25	52	23	40	80	7	1170
164	Rock Cornish Game Hens with Wild Rice	987	90	54	42	39	268	2	966
167	Flounder Florentine	430	36	17	24	50	84	2	913
168	Broiled Grouper with Tomato and Herbs	289	24	7	19	58	89	1	231
168	Cracker Crumb Fried Grouper[2]	364	53	17	7	19	130	1	245
169	Mahi Mahi Satay	419	36	17	25	52	83	4	4266
169	Mahi Mahi with Mango Salsa	398	36	62	3	6	132	8	166
170	Baked Whole Red Snapper	379	64	3	10	25	129	<1	197
171	Red Snapper/Black Bean Salsa	344	41	23	10	26	64	5	348
172	Salmon with Lemon and Dill Sauce	279	33	2	15	48	105	<1	139
173	Grilled Swordfish with Salsa Fresca	462	24	18	33	64	45	2	121
173	Salsa Fresca	196	3	42	4	18	0	5	41
174	Swordfish with Red Pepper Sauce	376	47	6	17	42	91	1	417
175	Florida Yellowfin Tuna Ragout	260	29	10	9	33	45	3	87
176	Crab Cakes	214	19	8	12	49	149	<1	690
177	Mrs. Thomas A. Edison's Deviled Crab	344	15	15	25	65	185	1	667
177	Baked Lobster	255	26	3	15	55	126	<1	900
178	Scallops Oriental	212	25	16	5	22	48	<1	749
178	Scallops with Green Herbs	329	19	4	27	72	98	<1	470
179	Shrimp Bernese	299	29	14	14	41	269	1	605
180	Shrimp Boil	375	30	35	13	32	218	4	2381
180	Charleston-Style Shrimp Curry	394	27	6	29	67	334	1	494
181	Jumbo Shrimp with Chive Butter	327	9	2	32	88	153	<1	660

Pg #	Recipe Title (Approx Per Serving)	Cal	Prot (g)	Carbo (g)	T Fat (g)	% Cal from Fat	Chol (mg)	Fiber (g)	Sod (mg)
181	Savory Shrimp	526	29	7	43	73	325	1	836
182	Marinated Grilled Shrimp with Tarragon	188	26	1	8	40	237	<1	546
182	Shrimp Remoulade	440	19	7	38	76	158	3	448
183	Fusilli with Seafood Sauce	692	33	79	26	33	35	8	268
184	Linguini with Clam and Shrimp Sauce	412	31	45	9	20	176	2	533
184	Penne and Sun-Dried Tomatoes with Tuna	467	37	50	13	25	47	4	638
185	Shrimp and Mushroom Fettucini	1195	40	93	74	56	494	4	592
186	South Florida Seafood Pasta	830	37	63	47	51	237	2	440
187	Spicy Basil and Scallop Linguini	295	19	39	6	17	24	2	572
188	Spicy Lobster Pasta	698	32	71	30	39	153	3	2177
191	Bread Pudding with Whiskey Sauce	786	13	127	24	27	154	3	607
192	Baked Apples	132	2	28	2	12	0	2	129
192	Chocolate Decadence	489	5	24	44	77	189	2	40
193	Chocolate Orange Mousse	489	8	33	40	69	294	3	63
194	Cream-Filled Eclairs	153	2	18	8	47	39	<1	164
195	Pavlova	483	5	53	30	54	109	3	70
196	Cherry Champagne Ice	227	1	51	<1	1	0	1	7
197	Mango Sherbet	195	2	48	1	2	1	1	45
197	Low-Fat Raspberry Cheesecake Parfaits	161	7	26	3	19	16	1	220
198	Orange Cream in Orange Cups	367	4	43	20	46	71	3	24
199	Strawberries with Grand Marnier	342	2	25	22	57	82	2	24
199	Tropical Sundaes	203	2	51	1	6	0	7	6
200	White Chocolate Mousse with Frangelico	415	5	27	31	66	185	0	65
201	Blueberry Cake	656	7	65	42	57	197	2	240
202	Toasted Coconut Cake	522	5	67	27	46	77	3	391
203	Glazed Fudge Cake	577	5	49	42	62	130	3	295
204	Hot Fudge Pudding Cake	271	3	51	8	25	19	2	210
205	Mango Cake	391	5	57	17	39	62	2	228
206	Pineapple and Carrot Cake	684	6	86	37	47	85	2	401
207	White Chocolate Cake	596	7	63	37	54	146	3	353
208	Pecan Pralines	148	1	17	9	53	9	1	7
208	No-Bake Citrus Bites	62	<1	9	3	39	3	<1	26
209	Rum Balls	83	1	12	3	35	3	<1	16
209	Fudgy Raspberry Brownies	86	2	16	1	15	<1	1	88
210	Glazed Key Lime Cookies	59	1	5	4	59	18	<1	2
211	Mocha Chocolate Chip Cookies	69	1	9	4	49	14	1	31
212	Frosted Orange Cream Chip Cookies	87	1	11	5	49	9	<1	26
213	Spiced Rum Ginger Cookies	51	<1	5	3	46	7	<1	<1

Pg #	Recipe Title (Approx Per Serving)	Cal	Prot (g)	Carbo (g)	T Fat (g)	% Cal from Fat	Chol (mg)	Fiber (g)	Sod (mg)
213	Santa's Whisker Cookies	80	1	10	4	46	8	<1	32
214	White Chocolate Almond Balls	127	2	13	8	56	11	1	35
215	Paper Bag Apple Pie	573	4	84	26	40	1	2	403
216	Coconut Cream Pie	351	6	45	17	42	85	2	243
217	Classic Key Lime Pie	372	9	52	15	35	123	<1	216
218	Low-Fat Key Lime Pie	325	8	50	11	30	4	1	370
219	Plum Tart	352	4	56	14	34	84	2	59
220	Strawberry and Kiwifruit Tart	318	5	35	18	50	59	3	140

Nutritional information for restaurant recipes is not available.
[1]Nutritional information does not include Colo Lopez.
[2]Nutritional information does not include oil for frying.

Suggestions for Healthier Cooking

*Try some of these suggestions to make your recipes more healthful, keeping
in mind that not all substitutions will work equally well in
all recipes. As with all your cooking endeavors, experiment and be creative.
You will be pleasantly surprised with the results.*

SUBSTITUTE	FOR
Skim milk	Milk or cream
Puréed fruit	Shortening or oil in baking
Part whole wheat flour	All-purpose flour
Defatted chicken or vegetable broth	Oil in sautéing
Drained nonfat yogurt	Sour cream
Nonfat cream cheese	Cream cheese
2 egg whites or egg substitute	1 egg
3/4 cup canola oil	1 cup margarine
2 1/4 teaspoons canola oil	1 tablespoon margarine
Canadian bacon or imitation bacon	Bacon
Ground turkey breast or tofu	Ground beef
Wine or broth sauces	Cream or butter sauces
Fat-free cheese	Cheese
Nonstick vegetable spray	Butter or oil
Herbs and spices	Salt
Fat-free cookie crumbs	Pie shells

Index of Recipe Contributors

Sheryl Wright Jones
Denise Barrington Joyce
Teri Karp
Margot Kenzie
Mary D. Kiefert
Kimberly Kuhn
Lara W. Kunkler
Martha M. Lambert
Jill Langella
Trish Leahy
Amye Lewis
Maggi Lewis
Linda Linnehan
John Lovelace
Kim Macdermott
Lisa Madden
Marie W. Mahan
Beth Martin
Keith May
Sharon McAllister
Rebecca McAlpine
Kerry McGuire
Brenda McKenzie
Kathy M. McKinlay
Cindy Meehan
Crystal K. Miller
Nan H. Miller
Emilie Moore
Janet Moore
Louetta Holst Muller
Gretchen Nelson
Gretchen M. Nelson
Janet Newman
Lori Nichols
Bunny Barker Nocera
Cynthia Nunez Niedert
Sandy Oss
Carol Ann Osterhout
Tammy Owins
Debbie Padnuk
Diane Coolman Page
Donna Pankow
Rose Mary Pfeffer
Erika Widen Pierce
Susan Holland Piotrowski
Nicole Pleasants-Lane
Valerie Pokorny-McHugh
Lou Turner Pontius
Kim Prather
Ashlyn Delaney Pratt

Sherry Priester
Sandra Kaye Raak
Sady Rademaker
Beth Marshall Ramsay
Anne D. Randolph
Lori L. Ravitz
Marycarol T. Reilly
Jeanie Richards
Cindy Roberts
Janice A. Roberts
Glynnis Fulton Rogero
Kimberly Rollick
Mary Burns Royal
Debbie Rynearson
Eloise R. Sarlo
Patricia Schaefer
Janet Schappell
Carolyn L. Shoemaker
Connie Cabana Sims
Gini Smith
Marlene Smith
Lisa B. Spearman
Ann Marie Spielmaker
Victoria B. Stephan
Barbara Stewart
Sheron Still-Weller
Stacy A. Stillman
Kathy Sturgis
Amy W. Stonner
Antoinette Giglio Swanson
Beth Swift
Denise Taylor
Cynthia Terry
Susan H. Tew
Charlene K. Timothy
Whitney A. Tinsley
Mary Lynn Trowbridge
Linda Uhler
Dolly Bymakos Usberghi
Beth Waldrop
Cynthia H. Weaver
Wendy Webb
Sherry Weeks
Janet Wenzel
Michelle M. Whery
Regina Williams-Erickson
Kathleen Williamson
Silvia M. Williamson
Bonnie L. Wiles
Janice L. Wolf

Index of Recipe Testers

Sherry L. Anderson
Sarah V. Andrew
Rebecca Antonucci
Ann M. Arnall
Lynn Arnold
Cheryl Arthur
Maureen D. Arnold
Sandra M. Atchison
Mary Ann Atherton
Deborah Azis
Vicki Royer Bachmann
Geralynn Barrette
Stephanie Bass
Linda Bateman
Kimberley B. Bauman
Victoria P. Bedford
Kathleen M. Berlick
Wendy Beville
Beth Bidgood
Donna B. Bowman
Alexandra Ross Bremner
Andrea Brody
Catherine Moushey Brooks
Jennifer Brown
Sandra Kolar Brown
Stacy Brown
Debbie N. Bubley
Anne Campbell
Jan Campbell
Annette Capel
Denise Carlin
Suzanne Brinson Clapp
Julia Clark
Patricia W. Clark
Kim J. Clause
Caryle Lyne Myosky Clyatt
Anne B. Cole
Melissa Congress
Carla R. Conkey
Regina Constantino
Peggy Coulter-Bos
Pamela Lynch Cramer
Jeana Feazell Crevasse
Helen B. Crumbie
Nan Dean
Nina Diamond
Julie Diehl
Linda A. Nicholas-Dombkowski
Michelle H. Dunham
Patricia McCleary Elkin

Kathy Eskin
Beth Stevenson Finstrom
Julie Dean Fisher
Andrea R. Fraser
Lisa Friedman
Jan Fryzel
Jamie Galeana
Betty Ann Galban
Lee Parker Gilmore
Renee Gipson
Lynn A. Girardin
Karen Adkins Globetti
Katherine C. Goenaga
Judy Goldstein
Sandra Greenberg
Pamela A. Gross
Sharon Gunsett-Kennedy
Myra P. Hale
Laura E. Hamel
Barbara Hansen
Suzanne Harris
Jody Hart
Jan Harvey
Lisa R. Hendry
Jackie N. Henricks
Phyllis J. Holley
Lori M. Houchin
Jacqueline A. House
Laurie Peters Hume
Kimberly K. Hunt
Jane Johnson
Betsi Jones
Sheryl Wright Jones
Denise Barrington Joyce
Teri Karp
Margot Kenzie
Mary D. Kiefert
Kimberly Kuhn
Lara W. Kunkler
Martha M. Lambert
Jill Langella
Trish Leahy
Amye Lewis
Maggi Lewis
Linda Linnehan
Marie W. Mahan
Beth Martin
Sharon McAllister
Kerry McGuire
Brenda McKenzie

Kathy M. McKinlay
Crystal K. Miller
Nan H. Miller
Emilie Moore
Janet Moore
Louetta Holst Muller
Gretchen Nelson
Gretchen M. Nelson
Janet Newman
Lori Nichols
Bunny Barker Nocera
Cynthia Nunez Niedert
Carol Ann Osterhout
Debbie Padnuk
Diane Coolman Page
Donna Pankow
Rose Mary Pfeffer
Erika Widen Pierce
Susan Holland Piotrowski
Nicole Pleasants-Lane
Valerie Pokorny-McHugh
Lou Turner Pontius
Kim Prather
Ashlyn Delaney Pratt
Sherry Priester
Sandra Kaye Raak
Sandy Rademaker
Beth Marshall Ramsay
Anne D. Randolph
Lori L. Ravitz
Marycarol T. Reilly
Jeanie Richards
Cindy Roberts
Jance A. Roberts
Glynnis Fulton Rogero

Mary Burns Royal
Debbie Rynearson
Eloise R. Sarlo
Patricia Schaefer
Janet Schappell
Carolyn L. Shoemaker
Connie Cabana Sims
Gini Smith
Marlene Smith
Lisa B. Spearman
Ann Maire Spielmaker
Victoria B. Stephan
Sheron Still-Weller
Stacy A. Stillman
Amy W. Stonner
Kathy Sturgis
Antoinette Giglio Swanson
Beth Swift
Cynthia Terry
Susan H. Tew
Charlene K. Timothy
Whitney A. Tinsley
Mary Lynn Trowbridge
Dolly Bymakos Usberghi
Beth Waldrop
Cynthia H. Weaver
Sherry Weeks
Janet Wenzel
Michelle M. Wherry
Regina Williams-Erickson
Kathleen Williamson
Silvia M. Williamson
Bonnie L. Wiles
Janice L. Wolf

Index of Recipes

Order Information

Tropical Settings
Junior League of Ft. Myers, Inc.
Cookbook Sales
P.O. Box 07341
Ft. Myers, Florida 33919
941-433-2440

Please send me _____ copies of **Tropical Settings** $19.95 each $ _____

Shipping and Handling $ 4.00 each $ _____

Gift Wrap $ 1.50 each $ _____

Florida Residents Add 6% Sales Tax $ _____

Total $ _____

Please make checks payable to: Junior League of Ft. Myers, Inc.

Name: _____

Address: _____

City: _____ State: _____ Zip: _____

Tropical Settings
Junior League of Ft. Myers, Inc.
Cookbook Sales
P.O. Box 07341
Ft. Myers, Florida 33919
941-433-2440

Please send me _____ copies of **Tropical Settings** $19.95 each $ _____

Shipping and Handling $ 4.00 each $ _____

Gift Wrap $ 1.50 each $ _____

Florida Residents Add 6% Sales Tax $ _____

Total $ _____

Please make checks payable to: Junior League of Ft. Myers, Inc.

Name: _____

Address: _____

City: _____ State: _____ Zip: _____